The Scruffy Martyr

and the

Resplendent Gentleman

iii

The Scruffy Martyr

and the

Resplendent Gentleman

Wilson McOrist

I suppose I have to dedicate this book to my bosom buddy and paddling partner, Brian Patrick Rock. (Only he knows whether this is a 100% true story, or one that has been embellished, slightly.)

The cover paintings and all drawings are by my highly talented brother, Ian Ferguson McOrist.

ISBN: 978-0-646-92258-4

First Edition, 2014

Published by the author
1 Williams Rd, Bonville, NSW 2450
Wilson.mcorist@gmail.com
www.kayakthemurray.com

Contents

Preface:

In Australian history, the names of Hume and Hovell are invariably linked together. These two explorers were the first 'non-locals' to sight the mighty Murray River, in 1824.

However, they were not a jolly pair of travellers, having many an argument on their travels, and afterwards. Hume was a tad upset that the public saw him as a *'subordinate to Captain Hovell'*. In Hume's opinion *'the expedition of 1824 was led and conducted by me'*, and that *'it was I who took him ... and brought him back again'*.

Another famous explorer Captain Charles Sturt conducted a number of expeditions on the east coast of Australia in the early 1800s. In contrast to Hume and Hovell, Sturt and his right-hand man & companion, a Mr. George M'Leay, had a ball together. For example, Sturt tells us that he enjoyed *'M'Leay's extreme good humour'*, he was impressed by M'Leay's *'indefatigable pursuit after subjects of natural history'*, and that M'Leay, seeing that Sturt *'was in considerable pain'* one day (from a mere toothache I may add), took over a few of Sturt's normal duties.

On one adventure together, Sturt and M'Leay boated their way down the Murrumbidgee River, met the Murray, and then followed it for 1240 kilometres, all the way to the sea, where the town of Goolwa in South Australia stands today. Sturt, M'Leay and their hardy men returned by slogging their way back up these rivers until they reached a few old horses they had left behind on the Yass Plains south of Sydney. From there it was a leisurely clip-clop into Sydney town on their trusty steeds. It was a journey that took six months.

1

When Sturt wrote up a detailed account of his expedition he described his motivation: '*it was simply with a view of laying the results before the geographical world*'.

Between 2006 and 2011, two old cronies kayaked down all of the Murray River: my good friend Brian Patrick Rock and me. When I decided to write up a detailed account of our 2500 kilometre journey I wanted to tell people we were a jolly pair of travellers, having nary an argument on our travels.

Hopefully you will agree with me that that Brian was forever taken with my '*extreme good humour*', just as I was mightily impressed with his '*indefatigable pursuit after subjects of natural history*'.

It may be open to conjecture as to whether Brian was subordinate to me, or visa-versa. That is, was our journey '*led and conducted by me*', or by Brian?

However, I am reasonably optimistic you will see that it '*was I who took him ... and brought him back*', not the other way around; but you be the judge.

The map here shows our travels, spread over six years.

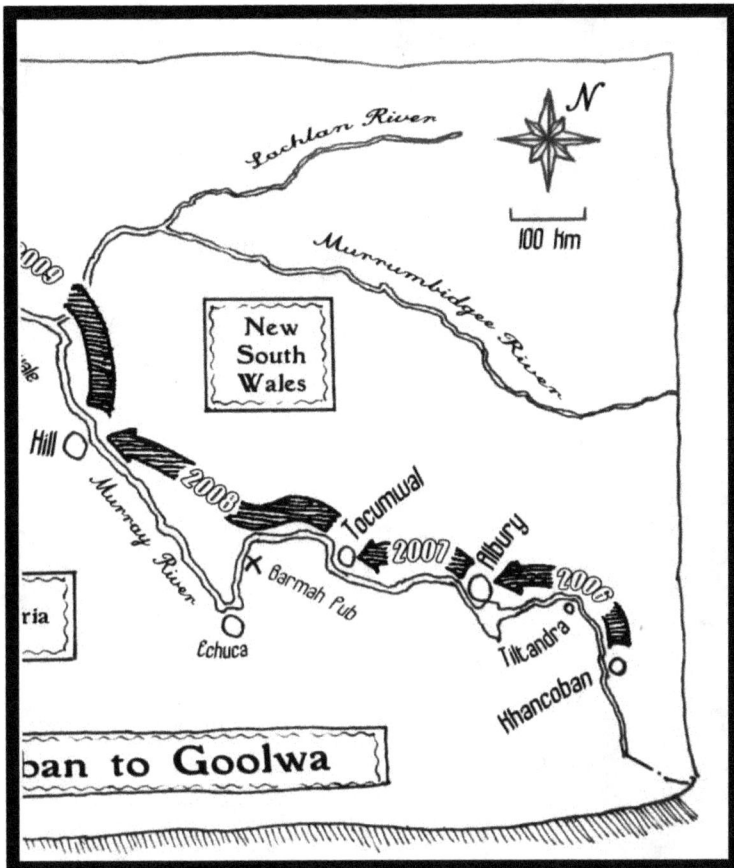

We started up near the source of the Murray, in 2006, and reached Albury that year. The next year we covered another 350 kilometres, from Albury to Tocumwal. Then in 2008 we managed 500 kilometres to reach Swan Hill, followed by another 500 or so in 2009 to arrive at Mildura. Personal circumstances made 2010 a rest year but in 2011, swept along by a flooded river we beached near Tailem Bend, this last leg being 888 kilometres.

Chapter 1: 'I need a pick-me-up'

[We meet my good friend Brian. We also are introduced to the Murray River and its explorers of the early 1800s. I buy a kayak.]

Brian Patrick Rock and me

Men often make long-term friendships at a young age. I was seventeen when I met Brian Patrick Rock, who was then fifteen, at the far from salubrious Montmorency Tennis Club, in a north-east suburb of Melbourne. We probably met on a Sunday. Sunday was a social mixed doubles day and we both went along for a hit of tennis, but as the years went by it was more of an excuse to chat with the girls, particularly a couple of twins Suzanne and Judith and two other sisters Sandra and Maxine. The chatting must have worked as I married Suzanne and Brian married Sandra.

Now, more than fifty years on, Brian and I are still close friends. Not that we saw a lot of each other over the years as we went our separate ways, Brian moved up to the back-blocks of north-east Victoria, near the Murray River, and Suzanne and I eventually settled in Coffs Harbour, 1000 kilometres away. As life went on we met once a year at best, but sometimes not even catching up for a few years. When either of us reached the magic age of 40, 50, or even 60 we did make the effort. Of course we were at each other's weddings, and I even went to Brian's second wedding to the second love of his life, Trish. He met her at Wodonga West High School, where he taught students the basics of geography, which for some inescapable reason focussed on research into marine life on the Murray River. The students were 'forced' to take numerous kayaking trips down the river with Mr. Rock, to learn the essentials of geography, like how to steer a kayak, put up a tent, bait a fishing line and how to lie to their parents on how intellectually stimulating these excursions were.

In a 2005 chin-wag he casually said to me:

"Wilson, I feel I need to do something more while I am still this side of the grave. I need a fillip, a sort of pick-me-up. Like taking a year off and traipsing around the vineyards of France, or taking a kayak trip down the Murray River and catching the largest Murray cod ever caught."

I was a little surprised he did not have higher ambitions - like wanting to spend a night with Angelina Jolie, or even two nights with Angelina - that would have set his old heart racing. But the chance of my school-teacher mate Brian seducing Angelina or any wild wenches was remote to say the least. He was not quite in the tall dark and handsome mould, more the shorter version, with a freckly, craggy, worn-out leather boot look of a face, a look he optimistically claimed was rugged. Plus, and more to the point, Angelina was probably never on his mind as he was living happily with Trish, his wife of twenty years.

If he ever went to France I would imagine he would buy an old 3-wheeled Citroen and visit winery after winery, wearing a beret and boring the pants off the locals laying claims to having produced Australia's best rough red - he did own a small vineyard at Barnawatha in north-east Victoria.

But France it was not to be because for some reason taking a kayak trip down the Murray River struck a chord with me. Here was the chance of a lifetime to live my dream: to be an old time explorer. As a boy I read about Sir Ernest Shackleton's epic boat journey of 1915, that ill-fated expedition when he and his men were stranded on the remote Elephant Island after their ship the *Endurance* was crushed by ice in Antarctica. I have been fascinated by the exploits of old-time explorers ever since. I even love Robert Falcon Scott, the notorious number one failed explorer who man-hauled his sledge to the South Pole with four others, and died on the way back. His final journal entries are compelling as he writes: *'right foot has gone; nearly all the toes ... Amputation is the least I can hope for now'*. For some obscure reason I was hooked on guys like Charles Doherty, a red headed Englishman who travelled in the deserts of Arabia in the 1870s and Wilfred Thesiger who enjoyed living off dates and brackish water as he too wandered across a desert or two in the last century. The Norwegian Fridtjof Nansen and his unsuccessful efforts to reach the North Pole in the 1890s fascinated me, as did Robert Peary's lifetime obsession to make that same place. I was also hooked on the adventures of Australian explorers, like Burke and Wills who in 1860 set off from Melbourne with the aim of being the first white men to traverse the Australian continent from south to north. They both died in the outback, in 1861.

Kayaking down a river

A boat journey down the Murray River would not be dangerous, and not exploring unknown waters of course but we would be away from civilisation for a while. I could even take

9

Scott's journals with me and read a few extracts to Brian. He would love them.

The more I thought about this trip down the Murray the better it seemed. As I kept thinking and thinking some more, pleasant pictures started to appear in my thoughts. I could see myself in a kayak, just slipping along like a sword-fish, touching the paddle here and there to take me around a bend. I could see myself resting on the river bank each night after a day of paddling; feet up on an old log, possibly a fishing line in the water to snare the evening's meal. The float bobbing and my eye-lids dropping, a beer in the left hand and a book in the right, dozing off now and again, sipping some more beer, just lazing the balmy evening away. I could see myself rolling out a sleeping bag of an evening on the river bank after billy-tea by the camp fire and looking up at the black night with a million stars winking at me. It just kept getting better and better.

So, out of interest, I wondered just how long this trip would take. Everyone in Australia knows the Murray: it is the country's second longest river after all, forming the border between New South Wales and Victoria as it travels west from Albury across to Mildura and flowing down into South Australia.

Where did the Murray River first bubble up? East of Albury was Lake Hume (created by the Hume Weir at Albury), and then the blue river line on the map I was perusing became thinner and thinner as my eyes followed it east and south-east upstream, through a few tiny dots of towns - Jingellic, Walwa and Tintaldra. Gradually the river line seemed to fade away into the Snowy Mountains, up near the Mount Kosciusko in the Kosciusko National Park.

So, to my eye, the start looked easy enough. All we would need is a couple of banjo playing hillbillies in the Tintaldra area to drop us up the river somewhere. Then we would paddle down to the Hume Weir at Albury where one of the mentioned hillbillies would have left our car, with engine intact, if we were lucky.

After Albury it all looked plain sailing - there were many good-sized towns along the way - Corowa, Yarrawonga, Tocumwal, Echuca, Swan Hill and Mildura. All this time the Murray was the border between Victoria and New South Wales. The Murray then moved into South Australia, and then headed north-west for a while to a place called Morgan way out in the back blocks. At Morgan the river quite rightly saw little value in continuing north-west towards the red-centre of Australia, so it did a sharp turn and dropped due south down to Murray Bridge, before entering Lake Alexandrina. At the end of the lake it sloshed out into the Great Australian Bight, in the Great Southern Ocean, near the town of Goolwa.

I worked out that a trip down the Murray, from its source in the foothills of Mt Kosciusko down to the mouth at Lake Alexandrina would be about 2500 kilometres. It would not quite be a Kon-Tiki trip from Peru, but it would be a challenge of sorts, and it did seem like a good idea at the time: a classic mid-life crisis concern that the mere male needs to raise his esteem in his own eyes.

If all else failed we would see far more of the Murray River than the well-known Australian explorers Hamilton Hume and William Hovell - famous for being the first white-eyes to see it, back in 1824. For Hume and Hovell only hopped across the Murray, once on their trip down from Sydney to the southern coast and then again on the way back. Not that they stayed long on the banks of the river on their return leg as they were itching to return to Sydney, no doubt to have their first hot bath for over three months. With six men, a few horses and a couple of carts being drawn by bullocks Hume and Hovell had left Sydney aiming for Western Port, the port in Bass Strait that George Bass discovered in 1798. Yet they somehow missed Port Phillip Bay, ending up near where Geelong is today, on Corio Bay, a little to the west.

Of all the old-time explorers, Captain Charles Sturt made the biggest contribution to actually charting the Murray. Here was a man Brian and I could compare notes with. Sturt was a man with quite a few famous expeditions under his belt. The one of interest to me, and to you, was his 1830 trip. On this occasion he left Sydney town with a small party of men and horsed and bullocked his way south-east to the Murrumbidgee River. Sturt then hopped in his boat, until then being towed in a dray, and his men rowed him down the point where the Murrumbidgee meets the Murray, about 160 kilometres downstream from where Swan Hill is today. He then followed the Murray all the way down to the sea, noting en route that the Darling River joined in along the way. Once he hit the sand banks by the sea, his men had to row (all the way back) upstream to reach their horses and then ride on to Sydney. Presumably the promise of a hot bath, like other explorers before them, was an allure.

If you would like to see the Murray River, you can take a scenic canoe trip at Walwa on the Upper Murray, or take a short cruise at Echuca on a Murray River Paddle Steamer. You can enjoy the peace and tranquillity on a luxury houseboat at Mildura, or even take a charter cruise in South Australia cruising past spectacular Red Gum forests and marvelling at the tall cliffs that tower across this stretch of the river.

But there is another way. If you can manage just a few weeks without immersing yourself in a tub of hot soapy water, and go without a few material comforts, you can kayak the whole length of the Murray River with a good friend; which is what interested me.

My charming wife Suzanne had doubts that I should even contemplate kayaking:

"Wilson, your old knees lock up when you travel in a car for an hour. What makes you think you could sit in a kayak and paddle, day after day? You've never even tried kayaking. Why not hire one for a few hours here in Coffs, and see how you go?"

12

But this sage advice I chose to ignore. Brian had suggested that we could do a few weeks and see where we got to, and then we could continue on from the same place the following year, if we wanted to. He told me we should start up near where the Murray has enough water depth for a kayak, beyond a place I did not know, Bridgenbrong Bridge, near a town I also did not know, Khancoban.

A kayak

Brian told me we would need two kayaks because he had tried kayaking in a double and he doubted we would make 100 kilometres being cooped up within half a metre of each other, let alone 2500 kilometres. We would need two cars to transport the kayaks because he knew that neither of our wives would be interested in being our supporting road crew; and we would need two tents because, apparently, he snored a little.

Of course my first task was to buy a kayak, so I visited a boating shop in town which was run by Doug and Vivien Gayford, a couple I knew. They were honest business folk and would guide me well. I stood inside the doorway of their showroom and looked around: the place would have been Mecca to a bona-fide boat-man as it was full of whopping-sized speed boats and wee little tinnies. You could buy rope that was as thick as your arm and strong enough to tow the Queen Mary. It was stock-in-trade to an old sea-dog but it was all too much for me; this was a speed boat shop, not a kayak shop and so I turned to leave.

But Doug caught my eye and, being the congenial sort of guy that all shop owners should be, asked if he could help. I was non-committal, telling him that I had just started a bit of research into the world of kayaks, because a friend and I were vaguely thinking of paddling down the Murray River. He led me down the back of his showroom where he stopped and pointed to a lonely looking canoe. Doug assured me, in his clubby cordial way that this was 'the boat' for me, a "Dagger

Edisto". To my eye the boat was a six-metre long, half-a-metre wide tube of blue plastic, with pointy bits at both ends and a hole in the middle with a little seat. I thought to myself: 'so this is a kayak', giving it a couple of authoritative taps with my knuckles as though I had inspected many kayaks before. This had little other effect than to move a layer of dust lying on the top. He told me it was 'a bargain' at $1,500.

This last required some deep thought - all of 20 seconds - then Doug had a sale, and so happy was he to have sealed the deal he even threw in a paddle. I was happy too, so happy in fact that I called Brian straight away to give him the good news.

Ominously, Brian's only reply was:

"I better buy the same model so we have similar kayaks, as I don't want to be going at twice your speed."

Chapter 2: 'A very fine river'

[Brian and I meet in Albury. We drive to Khancoban, where the river starts, for us. Our plan is to take two weeks to paddle the 350 kilometres back to Albury. Brian has a wardrobe of kayaking clothes. We meet a lady with long brown legs.]

I see the Murray River

So three months later there we were; two old buddies with two new kayaks, two cars and two tents standing outside the Newmarket Hotel in North Albury. Before we even inspected each other's kayak we were ready to start the trip with a celebratory drink. I decided that to commemorate the start of our epic journey we could have had our photo taken by the famous 'Hovell Tree' in the Albury Botanical gardens. In 1824, in the first known act of graffiti vandalism in this country, Hume and Hovell carved their initials in trees there. Only Hovell's tree still stands.

I also thought that dabbling our toes in the mighty Murray as it meandered through the centre of Albury, while sharing a bottle of champagne, might have been a good celebration point. We could have put our kayaks in there and headed downstream - it would have saved us a few hundred kilometres. Brian was not so impressed with this second idea of mine.

"Others claim to have kayaked the Murray," he said, "but most of them started below the Hume Weir. You and I will be starting up near the source, where the river is but a trickle, way up in the hills, three or four hundred kilometres from here. Then we can claim to have kayaked the entire river. Very few people can claim that."

I smiled at him. "I was jesting. Not a millimetre of the river will be skipped or missed."

As he went on to explain, not only would we be paddling each and every inch of the river, but we would also be doing this unsupported and unassisted. Apparently others who had kayaked parts or even most of the Murray had a support crew waiting for them each night with the tents up, tubs full of cold beer at the ready and steaks sizzling on the barbeque. Brian and I would be travelling without any helping hands.

A month before I had thought of selling my dear wife the idea that she could be our road crew and help out her husband in his once-in-a-life-time adventure. I had this vague notion that Suzanne may leap at the opportunity and that it would be real tonic for her; warm the cockles of her heart, that sort of thing. The proposal I thought of putting to her went along these lines: "My dear, the starting place for Brian and I is going to be up in the Snowy Mountains, where we can first get on the river. Would it be too much to ask for you to drive me down there? It is only a thousand kilometre trip, and we can have a romantic stay overnight somewhere halfway, like at a little Motel in Yass or Goulburn. You could then drive back to Coffs Harbour after dropping me and the kayak off and when Brian and I have coasted down to Albury, which should be after about two weeks, I will call you and you can pop down and pick me up. How does that sound?"

Then I thought - would she jump at the chance? I pictured her reading a book while I delivered my masterly sales pitch, followed by a brief lull in the conversation before she would most likely drop her chin down, slowly raise her eyes and give me a steely look over the top of her glasses to say something as brief and succinct as: "Take a wild guess." So I gave up on the idea of asking her.

So we had to leap frog the cars - we had no other option - a double drive and a paddle to move ourselves along each stretch of the river. My mind boggled at the thought of all this driving but I had guessed this is what we had to do.

Over a beer I made a toast to Brian that we would survive any black snake bites, brown snake bites, tiger snake bites, red-back spider poisoning, scorpions, food poisoning, starvation, dehydration, drowning, smashed up kayaks, holed kayaks, lost paddles and broken paddles. Brian added that there were no dangers up this way, apart from being raped by two sexy Swedish backpackers. The only thing for us to actively avoid was half submerged logs in the river. Getting caught on one could be dangerous: the weight of the entire river would be behind me so I should not prop sideways when resting up against a log - the force of the water could break my kayak in two.

He also warned me not to flip my kayak, which was a possibility if I was snagged by a tree. He reassured me that this could only happen in the first 50 or so kilometres where the current would be strong and the river quite narrow with some small rapids.

Our stage 1 plan, Brian's plan to be precise, being an experienced kayaker, was to drive east from Albury up to the start of the river near Khancoban, and come back in three hops; Khancoban to Tintaldra, about 100 kilometres, Tintaldra to Jingellic, another 50-100 kilometres and then Jingellic to

17

Albury, about 150 kilometres. He said we could leisurely do the first 'test paddle' from Khancoban to Tintaldra in three or four days, and for a beginner kayaker like me, it would be the perfect practice run.

We were finally away, heading east out of Albury in our two cars, with Brian's kayak on his car roof and mine on my trailer. I followed Brian as we drove: with our target the Snowy Mountains where the Murray would be but a mere stream. We were leaving civilisation behind for a while. East of Albury there is no river these days only Lake Hume, but after half an hour's drive we reached the end of the lake and the huge expanse of weir water changed into a fine river: the mighty Murray. There it was! It looked peaceful and serene as it snaked its way down through the countryside and we meandered upstream alongside. This was the Pacific Ocean of my own Kon-Tiki trip, I thought. Brian was more likely thinking of all the fish in there to catch. We then crossed over the river into NSW, and unlike the early explorers our passage was easy - some kind souls had built us a bridge. Our road then followed the Murray upstream even more closely, on the imaginatively named River Road. For a couple of hours we leisurely wended our way along, passing through grazing land and floating fields of crops waving at us in the breeze. The road was deserted, with not even a lone cow on the side of the road to watch out for, or to toot at.

Now back in the 1820s, the colonial Governor of the day, Sir Thomas Brisbane, was keen to see if there were any large or navigable rivers on the east coast of Australia. His initial thought was that an experienced bushman like Hamilton Hume could take a party of convicts down to the southern coast, by boat, and work their way back to Sydney, on the lookout for a river or two. However, it was decided instead that a party of men, under the command of Hume and William Hovell, would take an overland expedition starting from Sydney. Hume and Hovell kept a daily diary of their travels, but unfortunately Hume's diary was lost. However, some 30 years after their journey ended, Hume did write up a brief account, titled: *'Brief*

18

Statement of Fact, Etc, Etc. Expedition from Lake George to Port Phillip in 1824' and it was published in Melbourne, in *The Argus* newspaper, on Wednesday 9 May 1855.

Hume tells us of their start, where:

Mr Hovell agreed to meet me at my cottage at Appin. The party in all consisted of eight persons. We made our first start on the 3rd of October 1824.

In late November 1824, they first sighted the Murray, a little upstream from where Albury is today, and Hovell's journal entry for the day indicates it made quite an impression:

... we suddenly arrived at the bank of a very fine river, at least two hundred feet wide, apparently deep, with the bank about eight or nine feet above the level which is overflowed at the time of a flood, and the stream running about three knots per hour.

Hovell named the river 'Hume's River', since his companion Hume was the first to see it, but interestingly Hume later claimed that he named the river as a tribute to his father. But their naming of the river 'Hume' did not last, thanks to that other old-time explorer, Captain Charles Sturt.

Sturt was born in India, but he was educated in England where he obtained an Army commission and was promoted to Captain in 1825. He arrived in Sydney in 1827, where a good amount of the social chit-chat of the times surrounded the mysteries of inland Australia: then a great unknown. A number of rivers in NSW had been charted, indicating an inland sea in the centre of the continent. Sturt, along with some other budding explorers, was keen to throw his hat into the ring and find the sea, or at least work out where the rivers led.

Sturt lead two major expeditions into the interior. The first party in 1828 (which included our good friend Hamilton Hume), discovered and traced part of the Darling River. On his

19

second expedition Sturt followed the Murrumbidgee River, at first by horse, then in a whale-boat with seven of his men. On 14 January 1830 the Murrumbidgee carried them into the Murray, then called the Hume River. A few days later Sturt stood at the junction of the Darling River and the Hume and he decided to give his chances of Army promotion a kick along by re-naming the Hume, the Murray. This was in honour of Sir George Murray, secretary of state for all British colonies at the time, but Sturt's noble act did not help his promotion as much as he had hoped - a Captain he remained. Fortunately, Sturt was a man of many words and his field journals are full of edifying comments and interesting snippets of information. He wrote on everything, how they herded their horses and bullocks across rivers through to their encounters with the aboriginal population along the banks of the Murray.

The published account of his travels was horribly titled: *'Two expeditions into the interior of southern Australia during the years 1828,1829,1830,1831, with observations on the soil, climate and general resources of the Colony of New South Wales'.*

Driving to the Snowy Mountains

After a while Brian and I reached an up-country hillbilly town on the Murray River, Jingellic; a cool looking place with leafy trees along the sides of the road. It was not quite 'Deliverance' as neither of us had a banjo nor did we expect to meet any two-toothed hillbillies; but we did have a pair of kayaks.

We pulled up outside the Jingellic pub, a charming old weatherboard building with a blood-red corrugated iron roof and the same blood-red corrugated iron bull-nosed verandas. It overlooked the Murray, with a long expanse of green grass sloping down to the river. We found out that it was built in 1925 and laid claims to be the closest pub to the Murray River. That fact alone had to make it our new favourite pub.

Way down the road apiece I could make out a few houses but there did not seem a lot to little old Jingellic. In fact, with a population of only 50 or so, and apart from the pub, the general store, a few cottages and the riverside park, there is not a lot more to see. It is a small, quiet river community where the pub is the social centre of the area, so being sociable types we went inside.

After Jingellic we moved into the land known as Upper Murray River country and onto another peaceful town, Walwa, listening along the way to the local radio station 'Radio Upper Murray' - what else? We then whizzed through Tintaldra where the Tintaldra Hotel had that same blood-red corrugated iron roof. The local red-paint salesman must have had formidable sales skills - he had made a killing around these parts. We then rumbled over the delightfully named Bridgenbrong Bridge, and eventually reached Khancoban. I thought for a moment I could smell fresh mountain air which may have been stretching things a little, but I could see mountain backdrops in the distance. We had made it to the western slopes of the Snowy Mountains and Kosciuszko National Park.

Apparently Khancoban was first settled by Europeans in the 1830s, only a few years after Hume and Hovell first dabbled their toes in the Murray, 300 kilometres downstream. The families of Swampy Plains - as Khancoban used to be known - had a most peaceful life for 120 years distilling their own gin and swimming butt naked in the nearby (swampy) creek. "Why the name change?" I hear you ask. Well, firstly, as was common in those days, the settlers' huts were built by convicts and the convict overseers were named 'Coban'. Secondly, a couple of officers from the Indian army leased a run in the area in 1848 and 'Khan' means 'place' or 'hut' in India. These little snippets of trivia back up my case for explaining why the area became known as 'Coban's Khan'. Why the place then became 'Khancoban' I do not know, though possibly there were too many smarts cracks like, "Oh the Cobans can."

21

In any case the idyllic life of the Khancoban-ites was shattered in 1949 when construction began on the Snowy Mountains scheme, which aimed to divert water from the Snowy Mountains to produce electricity for the southeast of Australia. For 25 years, over 100,000 workers in hard hats wandered around digging holes, tunnels and aqueducts and occasionally whacking up the odd power station or two. 500 people live in Khancoban today, mostly employed in the nearby power stations. And to my knowledge these days most of the locals buy their gin from the bottle shop and wear Speedos if they swim, in the nearby Khancoban pondage created by the Khancoban weir.

I followed Brian's car through the town and into the Khancoban camping ground where we unloaded our kayaks, about to start our grand trip, on a balmy evening in early February 2006, at the south-western edge of the Snowy Mountains in the Kosciusko National Park. We proudly stared at our kayaks: Brian's a light blue puke colour which nicely complemented my dark blue puke coloured model. We walked around them a few times, giving each an assertive nudge with our foot before we put up our tents and agreed to have a meal at the local pub to save on our stock of kayaking food.

We celebrated the momentous occasion of finally reaching the start by knocking back a beer at the Khancoban Alpine Inn. We thought that with a name like the Alpine Inn it could well be full of those aforementioned Swedish backpackers, or failing that some hand-clapping Austrians swilling jugs of beer. The pub was classy, certainly compared to the Newmarket in Albury as it was built only fifty years ago for the workers on the Snowy Mountains project. Sadly we saw nobody that looked vaguely Austrian or any guys in hard hats, and there was not a Swedish backpacker in sight.

Packing the kayaks

The next day was day 1 for the river and both of us were feeling tip-top with anticipation. The first thing we did was to stand there and admire our two kayaks again, and a couple of little beauties they looked too. Through Brian's eyes they appeared long, sleek and built for speed while all I was thinking and praying was please be steady, stable and unsinkable. I gave my kayak a gentle touch with my toe; could this thing really transport me for two and a half thousand kilometres?

Brian was happy with the kayaks. Of course we could have gone for fibre glass models rather than moulded plastic ones, but plastic kayaks are far more rugged and less likely to puncture if we happened to run into the bank or scrape the bum on a half-submerged log. Seasoned pro Brian liked fibre glass kayaks as they were lighter, and faster, but we were in no rush. Or were we? Not me, that was for sure. I was looking just forward to a few days of easy paddling, letting the current push me along.

I knelt down and pressed on my seat, wondering if it would be comfortable enough. Up to then, I had paddled for no more than 30 minutes on the Bonville Creek at Coffs Harbour, but now we would be kayaking in them for days at a time. The seat was moulded plastic with a low back rest, but to my untrained eye it seemed okay - with a bit of bum and back padding provided by a loosely attached cover. The seat was well down inside the kayak so there was protection waist down from the sun, the wind and the water.

Inside the kayak at the front were two foot levers, one on each side with cables going back to the rudder. Press the right foot and the rudder pulled to the right, making the kayak go right. Press the left foot and the rudder pulled to the left, making the kayak go left. Soda! Steering should be a doddle, I thought.

My personal gear, apart from the clothes on my back - a T-shirt, football shorts, sandals and my straw hat - was an old pair of sandshoes, spare socks and jocks, another T-shirt, windcheater, track suit pants and a plastic rain jacket, not that I believed it ever rained up this way in February.

23

Brian had a little more kit than me - more like a wardrobe for a family of twelve - four different coloured shirts, short pants, long pants, dress shoes, $300 sneakers, a thick jumper, a thin jumper, a waterproof jacket, a windproof jacket and even a going-out-to-the-pub jacket. He held up a brown shirt and a blue shirt, like a salesman at a David Jones store, wondering which one matched his skin tone best.

I showed him my red plastic yellow-bladed paddle that I had been given by my friend Doug at the Coffs Harbour Boating shop. To my surprise, Brian was not impressed. "Cheap and nasty" were his exact words. Cheap it was - free even! Brian said my paddle looked more like a 'hire' paddle and come to think of it I did vaguely remember that Doug at the Coffs Boating shop also rented out canoes. Surely he would not have palmed me off with an old hire paddle? Surely not.

As a surprise for Brian, I had brought along two fold-up camp chairs, knowing from my camping days how unpleasant it could be to eat standing up, lying on the ground, or perched on a log.

He was impressed, and pleased, clapping his hands a few times. "Well, well, well those chairs are an excellent idea. So good you could knock me down with a feather."

"Some feather."

"I will ignore that smart crack," he replied. "These chairs are excellent! They are light and pocket-sized. They will be easy to transport on the top of the kayaks. Well done."

The day had started well. I had impressed the kayaking guru. He continued loading up his kayak and I lay down on the grass watching him. What was with the rush? It was a warm, sunny day and we were about to hit the river. Brian chatted away to me or to no one in particular, as he held up each item to decide whether to take it or not. I nodded and grunted at the right times, eyes heavy and head lolling, dozing off now and again as I watched the clouds rolling by. He put on his mosquito head cover, explaining how it fitted over his hat and covered all of his face, an essential item up this way. Another grunt from me did nothing to stop him talking.

Without a doubt, the early explorers packed lighter. As a rough example, for his party of eight men, the clothing Sturt listed in his journals was: '8 *Jackets. 8 Duck frocks. 8 Shirts. 16 Trousers. 24 Pair shoes and 16 Pair stockings.* (Stockings are socks to you and me). And, who in their right mind in 1830 would travel without a duck frock, which was a smock - like sort of long sleeved shirt with a bib. Even Brian was not into duck frocks. Hovell wrote that his men were provided with a '*suit of slops*' each - a great little description if ever I heard one – for loose cloth from the waist reaching just below the knee.

Hume and Hovell's men also carried a *'musket or fowling-piece plus many pounds of gunpowder and sixty rounds of ball cartridge'* and for bedding all they took was *'one blanket for each of the men, plus two tarpaulins, and one tent made of coarse Colonial woolen cloth'*. Brian and I were unarmed, except for Brian's fishing lines. We had the best sleeping bags money could buy, and, as you know, we had a tent each. In the 1820's the Government of the day also provided some items for Hume and Hovell's party, but Hume tells us that he:

had to dispose of a very fine imported iron plough (no small consideration in the days of which I speak) to help raise money sufficient to purchase supplies.

Long Brown Legs

Finally, my good friend was ready. We left the kayaks at the Khancoban camping ground and an hour later we had driven the 35 kilometres down to Tintaldra to drop off one of the cars. Brian assured me that at the Tintaldra pub they serve the best steaks in Victoria which we could look forward to after a few nights on the river.

I followed Brian into the 'The Clearwater', the Tintaldra Upper Murray Caravan Park. It was a peaceful looking, 'pets-allowed' park, so you could even bring in your own hairy-backed gorilla if you liked, if you had one. A rather charming looking lady walked out to greet us, wearing nothing but a T-shirt propped up on two long brown legs. Brian, usually quick to say a few words to anyone - particularly an attractive lady wearing nothing but a T-shirt propped up on long brown legs - suddenly had lock-jaw and just stood there, speechless.

"Hi," I said. "We are kayaking down the river from Khancoban. We plan to return here in a few days. Can we pay you to leave one of our cars here? We will also be camping here for a night when we do arrive."

The lady replied, "That's fine. Normally my husband would see you but he is not well at the moment."

I glanced at Brian and his jaw had dropped even further. I diagnosed a severe case of love at first sight lock-jaw. I moved across and lifted up his chin so he looked near to normal and suddenly he sprang into life by patting down his hair, drawing in his paunch and joining in the conversation.

"Hi. What a lovely place you have here. I'm teaching this old friend of mine how to kayak and I hope to have him back here in a few days, provided he listens to my instructions of course, because I'm actually a qualified kayaking instructor. What a lovely place you have here. Can you show me the amenities? My, what a lovely place you have here."

And off he went to look at the capacity of the washing machines, prancing around the lady, always making sure to be facing her so as to keep his thinning patch at the back of his head from her view. After a few minutes he returned, telling me:

"Can't just rush in and rush out. That's not the way we do things in the bush. We country folk always take time to get to know people and spend some time in idle chit-chat."

Then he added, "Anyway, I found out her husband is just having a rest in one of the back rooms, so it was time to leave."

As we drove past the Tintaldra pub on our way back to Khancoban Brian gleefully said: "Best steaks in Victoria. Can't wait to stroll in there in a few days time."

STAGE 1:

2006. Our first ten days together

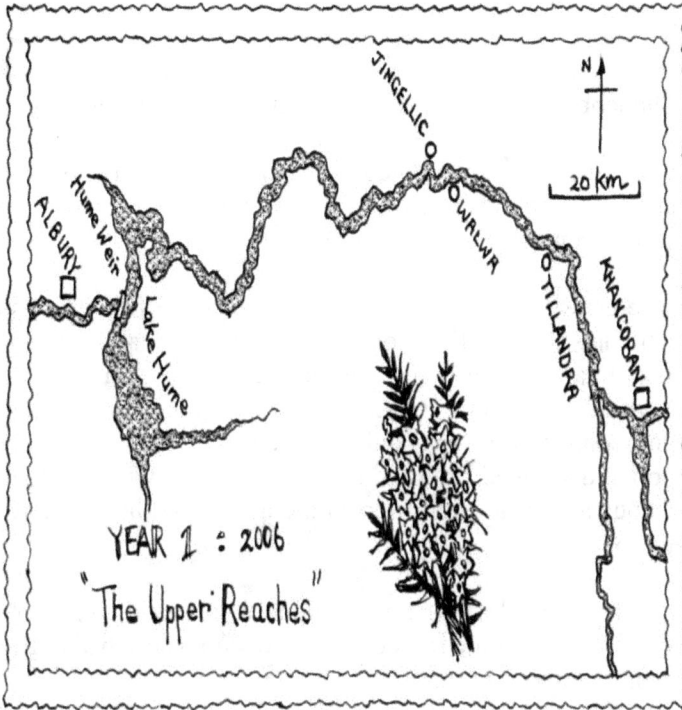

YEAR 1 : 2006
"The Upper Reaches"

Chapter 3: 'Rendered all the assistance'

[I have some difficulty in starting, and then kayaking around corners. We camp, our first night on the river bank. We eat our first, and not our last, meal of noodles.]

On the water

An hour later, now approaching mid-afternoon, we were back in Khancoban where we picked up the kayaks at the camping ground and dropped them down by the river's edge. The river surged, gurgled and bubbled past us - the water was being pumped out from the Khancoban Weir just upstream - there certainly seemed to be a strong current.

A large crowd had gathered to watch us as we fiddled around with the kayaks, but they soon returned to their labour of love; a perennial pastime of grass munching, miraculously converting grass into milk. We ignored them and tinkered around some more, repacked bits, tied the camping chairs on the top and slopped on more sun-block. Then, with a shake of the hands and a farewell moo to the assembled herd, we were set to go.

I pushed my kayak off the bank and took a careful step into the water, but it was a metre deep and I was up to my waist. Brian saw some humour in this.

"Now the first rule of kayaking is that you test the depth of the water before you step off the bank. That's one of the many uses of the paddle. Now you're in the water, how do you plan to get in the kayak?"

We pulled my kayak up onto the bank and I poured the water out of my pockets while Brian (politely) explained the recommended method for getting into a kayak; in deep water. I had to keep the kayak close to and parallel to the bank, use the paddle as a brace on the ground, place one leg into the kayak, slide one's backside into the seat, then bring in the second leg and then push off using the paddle. I listened (politely), then I hopped in on the solid ground and Brian pushed me into the water to get me started.

Away I went, bobbing and bobbling out to the centre of the river, then taken downstream at a jolly little rate of knots by the strong flow from the weir; but backwards. "Holy Cow!" I screamed to myself, I'm going backwards. "Holy Cow!" I screamed again, this time not just to myself. I did not have a clue where I was going.

On attempting to look around, I came close to flipping the kayak. I then tried some vigorous paddling on one side to turn myself around, but the kayak wouldn't turn so I continued to head downstream, backwards, at a great pace. Brian, now in his kayak, was closing in on me, which I could easily see, what with me facing backwards.

"Put down your rudder," he yelled.

"Rudder?"

Ah yes, the rudder! There were plastic knobs on each of the two rudder lines and I remembered somehow that when they were next to each other the rudder was up, so I pulled one, and this dropped the rudder into the water. I paddled like crazy to go clockwise, and pressed the foot rudder to help me turn clockwise, and slowly the kayak came around. Finally, I now faced the right way, downstream. I was away at last. I was now actually kayaking, flying along at a full lick. The journey had begun, beyond doubt.

"Woo-hoo. Man this is good," I yelled at Brian, just before I hurtled full pelt into a weeping willow tree on the left hand bank, as the river turned sharply to the right.

I shot straight through the willow, somehow hanging onto my hat and paddle, and found myself up against the left bank, stuck in the mud. I looked around and Brian was over the other side of the river in a tranquil patch of water on the inside of the bend. I pushed myself off the bank and paddled across to talk to him where he greeted me with a round of applause. No bugger had told me about bloody willow trees. I had imagined I could just sit in the middle of the current and go around the bends with the water flow.

"May I ask," said Brian trying hard not to smirk. "How did you handle the current around Bonville Creek?"

"Okay," he then said, with a dash of compassion (he genuinely is a considerate guy underneath that craggy, freckly face), "the best way to travel is for you to follow my lead, at least until you get the hang of it. Watch how I go around the bends and see how I paddle hard to avoid the current taking me into the trees."

Off we went again. At first the river was straight so I fairly flew along with no concerns, but after a few hundred metres the river narrowed and the current quickened. The river then turned to the right and I watched Brian keep a little towards left of centre of the river, pulling hard once he reached the bend to keep himself from going straight ahead into the trees on the left bank.

I must have overdone the paddling on the left side and/or the rudder push to go right as suddenly I went around in a circle, and scooted backwards across the river, straight towards the right bank, becoming becalmed. A series of little whirlpools, eddies or backflows had taken me there, but at least I hadn't crashed into the willows on the left bank.

I think Brian quite enjoyed my trials and tribulations. "This is fun and games. I didn't realise you would be so entertaining. I may have asked you this already, but have you ever kayaked before?"

Brian broke out into hoots of laughter followed by a coughing fit which brightened me up a little.

In the water

After a couple more bends I finally had the hang of it. If the river turned to the right I stayed only slightly left of the middle of the current and the other way when it went left. The straight stretches were a doddle. I now realised this kayaking lark was a bit of a breeze and I felt like a know-all paddler, just like my buddy 50 metres ahead.

But then the river turned sharp left again. Keep to the left of the middle, I thought or ... was it to the right of the middle? I panicked. I pulled hard on the right side to get in the left hand side of the river but I was too late - I went straight into a bunch of willow trees and possibly a submerged log or two, because before I knew it I was in the water. I had slammed into a log or a tree and it had flipped the kayak over, with me in it.

I surfaced, hanging onto my paddle and somehow also hanging onto the kayak which had righted itself. I crashed through the willows like a fun-park dodgem car, but then I was out of them, being swept down the river, quite helpless, but still clutching my kayak in one hand and my paddle in the other. Hang onto the kayak at all costs I thought, and I did, through a few more willows but fortunately not over any more submerged logs. The river finally widened and straightened up so the current dropped away which allowed me to swim by using sidekick across to a sand bank, hauling the kayak with one hand and the paddle with the other. I then collapsed, hatless, breathless, and one shoe less. At least I had my kayak and paddle.

Where was Brian? I looked around and there he was just behind me, sitting up in his kayak like a contented cat that has just licked up the spilt milk. He even had a Cheshire cat grin spread across his face.

"I didn't know whether to laugh or cry," he said. "Maybe it would have been better if you had drowned, but explaining how it happened with a straight face would have been hard. How are you by the way, apart from being wet?"

I ignored his quite clearly insincere question about my health and asked him: "Where are we getting to today? Tintaldra wasn't it? It is surely just around the corner."

"Not quite", he replied. "We have travelled not much more than one kilometre so there are ninety-nine to go. What I would suggest is that we find a ducky camping spot, put up the tents and you can light the camp fire and dry off while I catch us some fish for dinner."

Together we rolled over my kayak to get rid of some of the water and lo and behold my missing shoe came out with the water.

"Joy! I have two sodden shoes, all I need now is my hat."

And there it was, out in the middle of the river, my old straw hat, floating by like a match down a sewer pipe. So Brian, bless his little heart, paddled out to retrieve it. I was back to my former state of half-an-hour ago, bar being soaked and soggy.

I put on my sagging straw hat and we pushed off, with me mentally doubling up on my earlier statement to stay well clear of sunken trees, but now also on the lookout for a large cow or bull I could lasso to be pulled along. But the river remained quite easy - that is relatively straight and wide - for the next kilometre. Eventually Brian selected a camping spot, so we pulled in, dragged our kayaks up on the bank and sat on the grass. I looked around again for the nearest cow and Brian looked for a suitable fishing spot.

No broken frying pans for us

Now even after my river dunking, and Brian's obvious delight in seeing me go under, I had this crazy notion that no matter what happened on our trip, Brian and I would remain brothers-in-arms, birds of a feather, thick as thieves. Unlike Hume and Hovell I should add. These two lads did not seem to have a jolly old time when travelling together, and certainly didn't remain friends afterwards; possibly because they came from different sides of the track. Hume was a true blue Australian, born near Parramatta in New South Wales, but as his father was a convict overseer he did not enjoy a high social standing. Hovell, however, was born in England, he had commanded ships and married a surgeon's daughter, before eventually settling on land near Sydney.

Thirty years after their expedition Hume wrote in his report that he was none-too-happy that Hovell received all the adulation after their joint efforts. Hume said:

I have felt roused, somewhat chagrined, to find that Mr. Hovell has somewhat monopolised, with the public, the fame and credit of the expedition to Port Phillip, that he was associated with myself in 1824.

I made a mental note never to become chagrined if my fellow-traveller Brian received as much public adulation, fame and credit as me, after our journey was over (even if he did deserve as much).

To Hume, he was the hero:

with a fixed determination to go on and if he had not we would not have reached the south coast ... if he had yielded in the least to the reluctance of Mr. Hovell ... our expedition must have ended on the north bank' of the Murray.

I made a mental note never to be kayaking with 'reluctance', and further more to do so with a 'fixed determination'.

These two Australian heroes (Hume and Hovell, not McOrist and Rock) had many arguments. Once they were up in the Snowy Mountains near the Tumut River, arguing over which course to travel, so they separated. Before parting they even had a row over who should keep their frying pan, and ending up breaking it in two by pulling at it. Oh to be a fly on a gum leaf watching that! I made yet another vow to give Brian the frying pan if we go separate ways, I could find a pub for my meals.

On another occasion, arguing again over which course to follow and deciding to part ways, they had a row over who was to have the tent, even contemplating cutting it in two. This wouldn't pose a problem for Brian and I - we had a tent each. Hume wrote that '*after the rupture*' they rejoined forces and travelled together. I made another mental note – if Brian and I have a disagreement I won't call it a blue, a brawl, or a broil, but a 'rupture'. I like that word. Much more civilised.

What really ticked Hume off was all the kudos Hovell received when their travels were over. Hume was a tad hot under the collar that Hovell, his: '*quondam fellow-traveller... ended up enjoying more than a lion's share of starring*'.

Of course Hovell disputed all these accusations, stating that he ' *rendered all the assistance I thought necessary.*'

One can only guess that Hume won the argument in the long term, as we now have the 900 kilometre Hume Highway between Sydney and Melbourne - compared to a couple of meagre William Hovell roads, in the city of Canberra and the town of Seymour.

Peanuts and Guinness

As we put up our tents, I noticed a small rip in the floor of mine but there was nothing I could do. Brian shook out his automatic-just-unroll-and-it-inflates mattress while I laboriously pumped up my lilo using a foot pump and then we unrolled our sleeping bags. Brian's was designed for minus five degrees centigrade temperatures – "it can get cold up here at night", he told me - which I doubted would be the case as we were travelling in the middle of summer. He also had a pillow made of down so he could roll it up into a small ball when packing it away; a head-light (just like a coal-miner, he claimed), a large torch and six packets of batteries, a small camp lantern (we would be lit up like a Xmas tree at night); a deluxe campers face washer and a deluxe campers towel made of a fast drying fabric; binoculars so he could look at the feathered birds in the sky and non-feathered birds swimming naked in the river; and a compass. I did think of asking him why we needed a compass when we only had one road to follow, the river, and it was a one way road, downstream. I could not see us ever getting off the river, except to visit a shop, or a pub.

Brian had also brought his fishing gear, a coffee maker, a four-can pack of Guinness and a cask of red wine. Now some of these items seemed sensible, like the Guinness, most appropriate, and the cask of red wine, eminently sensible.

Our campsite was on a flat grassy area in an out-of-sight farmer's cow paddock, the perfect spot for me to lie down, rest and await the big game hunter to bring in the brace of fish. It was already after five, and I was happy to have stopped for the day – not only had we made it onto the river, but I had made it into the river.

An hour later Brian returned, noticeably without a school of fish dangling on a pole over his left shoulder, Tom Sawyer style, so I offered him prawn noodles for dinner.

So on a warm, windless evening we relaxed in our new camping chairs like a couple of geriatrics, throwing peanut shells in the fire and sipping on Guinness. Apart from the odd fly, no doubt attracted to this area by the pads of cow poo everywhere, this place made for a perfect camp site, with soft lush grass under our feet and the river lapping softy close by.

Back in 1824 peanuts and Guinness were not on the menu. Hovell tells us they lugged along stacks of flour, salt, tea and coffee, and '*three hundred and fifty pounds of pork.*'

Sturt on his travels a few years later also took along some sheep, obviously well before he launched his boat. He noted that '*sheep gave little additional trouble only that they had to be penned up at night to protect them from the aborigine's dogs.*'

Best of all was that they could whip up a lamb stew once a week, a necessary and wholesome change of fresh food from the diet on which they usually lived.

Sturt even took along a 1800s water purifier, for he was a thorough man and keen to provide for every contingency on his expeditions. He had cleverly constructed a small still for the distillation of water, just in case he found the river waters salty.

Noodles and coffee

Cooking noodles does not require a lot of talent: 'Open up to the dotted line. Add flavour and vegetable sachets. Add boiling water to fill. Close lid for two minutes. Remove lid and stir with fork provided. Enjoy straight from the cup'. An easy job, even for a couple of old kayakers!

An hour later Brian prepared us a coffee on his 'Bialetti' espresso maker, then he went off fishing. I lay there in my tent listening to him sloshing around in the shallows, watching his head-light swirl around breaking up the black of the night and hearing him cursing and cussing now and again when he caught a carp. Brian did not eat carp, but he took great delight in killing them, by belting them with a rock. "You bastard, take that, and that!" rang out in the darkness, no doubt causing great concern to the locals trying to sleep. By locals I mean the assembled owls and wombats. Apparently it is illegal to return carp to the water, or so he told me.

Eventually I dozed off into the land of Nod, dreaming of a plate of Murray cod for breakfast but in the middle of the night I was snapped wide awake, by a soft rustle in the undergrowth next to my tent. I then remembered a story in a primary school reading book about a boy who wakes up with a snake on his stomach. What if a snake came through that rip in the floor of the tent? Breaking out in a cold sweat, I leapt up, found a sock and stuffed it into the rip. After that little drama, it took me some time to get back to sleep. At some ungodly hour in the early morning Brian's words 'it can get cold on the river at night' came back to haunt me. I slipped into my sleeping bag first of all, then it got colder so I put on a T-shirt but then colder still and before long I had on my windcheater, track suit pants, and a single sock. By early morning my teeth were chattering away as I lay there shivering. The mongrel was right; it can get cold on the river at night.

I would like to make mention here that our other old time explorers, Hume and Hovell also complained about the cold: *'this morning the weather was very cold, so much so that we could not keep ourselves warm in bed, and with all the clothes we could put on us.'* I could relate to that.

Pancakes

Just after daylight Brian was back down at the river bank, casting his line in, reeling it back, putting on some new bait, casting it out, reeling it in, and putting on some new bait, casting out. Ah, the simple pleasures in life for my friend, the fisherman.

He had slept well - it was all down to his down pillow – what had I used for a pillow he wondered? I explained that I used my windcheater at first but once I'd put that on to keep warm, I used a shoe inside my tent carry bag. Ever the resourceful camper!

I decided we would have pancakes and maple syrup for breakfast, but somehow I had forgotten to buy any oil, so we tried poaching them which resulted in a sort of witches brew, a goulash with globs of white goo floating on murky water. I had never seen curds-in-whey but my guess is that pancake mix in water is what curds-in-whey would look like. They were inedible, looking and tasting like stale flour in water.

Flour was a talking point for the early explorers too, who were shown by the aborigines a way to produce it, which may well produce tastier pancakes than ours. They took up a root of a large reed or bulrush which grew in a dry lagoon and extracted from it rhizome - a quantity of gluten. The root of the bulrush was cut into lengths of about eight or ten inches; the outer rind peeled off and laid in front of a fire, then it was twisted to loosen the fibres and lo and behold a quantity of gluten, exactly resembling wheaten flour - to the white-eyed guys of the 1800s - was shaken out. Many an old-time explorer was impressed by this, seeing that this gluten, which the aborigines called 'Balyan', must be an essential part of their diet.

Chapter 4: 'No meals tonight mate'

[I manage to stay upright for the day. I find out we were not on the Murray. Kayaking becomes pleasurable. We reach Tintaldra, 100 kilometres from Khancoban, but a thick rump steak at the pub is hard to come by.]

Kayaking

I told myself to forget yesterday. Today would be my first real kayaking day.

Brian told me to stick twenty or so metres behind him as there were a few small rapids in the next stretch of river and a few sharp bends where the current could drag me into the bank if I was not careful. I would be careful, trust me. Brian called them grade one and grade two rapids, so I should have nothing to worry about *except* when the current flowed quickly around the bends where the river was narrow.

I kept thinking - do not capsize again today. "Concentrate," I told myself because it's not quite as simple as you thought this paddling lark. Concentrate I did, squinting ahead like a sniper to see how Brian tackled a bend, or which direction he took when the river split around an island. Staying sharp-eyed and single-minded, that was the key.

Once I got the hang of going around sharp bends without impaling myself on the bank or bulldozing through a willow tree it was quite enjoyable, maybe even more than quite enjoyable, it was most pleasant. On a warm sunny morning I felt like a K1 kayaker at the Olympics, zipping down the Upper Murray. Brian would get a bit ahead of me but then prop by the bank until I caught up, encouraging me: "Keep practising and you will become a perfect paddler."

Off he went again with me his faithful disciple following in his wake. The sun shone and it was warm but I kept myself cool with an accidental method - every stroke a few drops of water would fall off the paddle end up in the air and drip onto my head, shoulders arms and upper legs. Occasionally the river depth would become quite shallow when the river widened and our kayaks would scrape the pebbles or sand on the river floor. A few times we even had to get out and drag them in shallow places, but most of the time we just went with the flow,

45

cruising along in the middle of the river in the straight stretches and flying around the bends.

After an hour my backside started to ache and my knee had locked up (exactly as Suzanne had predicted I may add), so we pulled over so we could have a walk around, a shake of the legs and a rub of the buttocks. After the rest we continued on, bobbling along like a couple of corks. Brian managed to stay out of any trouble, whereas I said hello to a few willow trees when I was swept across the corner on some sharper bends.

After a second hour of paddling my backside and knee were again crying out for some activity, so I called for another rest. On the grassy bank I lay on my back, soaking up the sun shining at us over a hill's shoulder, dozing off and watching the occasional fish make a ripple or pop up and flop back into the water. Then my eyelids started to drop, and I was away in the land of soft women's breasts.

During the third hour of paddling I noticed a stream joining our river, from the left. Naturally I asked Brian what stream it was and he told me it was the Murray River. I was flabbergasted. He went on to tell me that up to now we had been on the Swampy Plains River, which like the Murray starts up in the Snowy Mountains; but now we would be on the Murray, all the way.

"How can I tell people I kayaked the Murray?" I said. "We've been on the wrong river!"

"Well the real Murray before this junction would have been useless for us; it's too shallow for our kayaks. We had a few options, the first to have two kayaks each, the other a white water kayak which we could have used to traverse the thirty klicks from the real start of the Murray to this spot, and then swap kayaks. Option two was to simply put our kayaks in at the Bridgenbrong Bridge, which you will see coming up soon, and option three was to start where we did at Khancoban, where there was a camping ground and a suitable place to leave the car and do ten kilometres to this junction. If anyone asks you, tell them you started at the start of the river. No one will ever know the difference, and it's only twenty kilometres difference anyway."

Shortly after getting on the right track, as in the right river, the *actual* Murray River, I saw the Bridgenbrong Bridge coming up. There we saw our first (brief) sign of civilisation since Khancoban as a car rumbled across, just before we peacefully paddled under.

"We could have started here," I said, "but there was nowhere to leave a car I suppose."

"Not to mention I would have missed seeing you flip over, which could well end up being the highlight of our trip."

Blissful Paddling

The Bridgenbrong Bridge was our last sign of human life for some time but we sure didn't miss it, enjoying three warm and windless days on an unspoilt, unsullied stretch of river. We gently paddled and then drifted, coasting with the flow, wending our way along like a couple of loafers. We simply dawdled, a pair of lazy-bones letting the current take us at its own speed, with some occasional fast paddling by me to avoid the willows.

We moseyed along through dead-quiet bush-land and past farmland with mud brown horses grazing and cattle chewing the cud. It was pristine. The cows always looked up at us as we drifted by but not the horses – they just blinked their big brown eyes and kept on nibbling without another care in the world. I wonder why - why do cows look up at you but horses don't? In the background at times we could see the mountains and sweeping views across the Murray River Valley. The scenery was fit for a picture postcard and the only signs of humans were an occasional corrugated tin shed or a dilapidated old farm house.

We gave away the pancake idea and breakfasted on tortilla bread and vegemite for three days, dilly-dallying around lighting the fire and having cups of tea, with Brian throwing his fishing line in, searching for that ever-elusive-catch of a lifetime.

We continued the easy pace through the day, often gliding past birds on sandbanks that padded and stabbed around in the shallows, watching us with a wary eye as they pecked their bent beaks into the sand in search of a tasty nibble.

When we drifted in shallow water Brian would point left and right and call out: "See the Cod down there? To the right. See those red fin? To the left. A school of them."

We slowly floated across clear water looking for fish and occasionally sloshed our way on foot in pebbly shallows and through foot-deep foaming rapids, dragging our kayaks.

We rounded bend after bend after bend, through deep ponds and shallow ponds, in crystal clear, crystal clean water. At times the river widened considerably and our paddles would scrape on the bottom, but when the river narrowed we met shallow rapids which we could see coming up by the rippling soft water foaming over the rocks.

The river seemed undisturbed, with gin clear, algae-absent water. Clusters of weeping willows and tall grasses lined the banks at the water's edge, broken here and there with patches of inviting grass. There were also pockets of medium sized gum trees, up to 20 or 30 metres in height together with baby gums, struggling their way up to join their mum and dad. The trees, the willows and the reeds formed a barrier to the cleared countryside alongside the river.

This area is known as the 'Upper Murray' and it felt untouched, except by mug kayakers like us. There were no houses for us to see, no other people in or by the river, not a human voice did we hear. The river drifted down a wide valley and in the distance away from the river we could see natural mountain bush land. It did not seem to have changed a lot since Banjo Paterson whipped up his famous poem, 'The Man From Snowy River' in 1890, which starts with:

He hails from Snowy River, up by Kosciusko's side, where the hills are twice as steep and twice as rough, where a horse's hoofs strike firelight from the flint stones every stride ...

Not that we were on the Snowy River (it started up near Mt Kosciusko like the Murray and went down the other side of the Snowy Mountains) but Banjo writes a good poem.

The trees would open up now and again and we would say hello to grass chomping cows that would turn and tread their way towards us, or simply raise their heads to give us a moo or two.

We always stopped every hour – my knee and bum demanded it. This hourly rest and recuperation continued for almost the entire trip. I needed it to knead my bum and flex my locked up knees. Our lunch break was just a longer break with some unleavened bread, cheese and sardines or tuna sometimes, with the added luxury of a fruit juice. We were at least eating fish, albeit tinned - and the oil would be good for the joints as by now they needed greasing up a little.

Our evening conversations were not full of wisdom but quite light, on the brink of being frothy. For example:

"Exquisite evening."

"Not bad."

"Charming camping spot."

"Not bad."

"Did you see that fish jump then?"

I shook my head. "No."

"I saw a wallaby at about four o'clock, did you see him?"

I nodded.

Back in 1824 when close by the Murray, Hovell noted in his journal that one day *'they met with a considerable number of native women and children, perhaps about thirty'.*

The children were engaged in play, throwing small spears, formed of reeds, at a circular piece of bark, about a foot in diameter, while it was rolling along the ground;

... the women were employed in spinning the native flax, one of whom, (an old woman,) gave immediate notice of their approach, crying out white man! white man! minija! minija!

(Note the women were working hard, as women do - but not the males apparently - as was the case then and many would claim is still the case today.)

The best steaks in Victoria

It's fair to say that Brian and I had quite different sleeping patterns. I would retire to my tent ten minutes after I had knocked off the nightly noodles, the ten minutes being enough for a polite chit-chat. I would lie there, hearing the fire crackling and listening to a silent world.

Silent but for the sloshing sound of Brian's boots in the shallows as he fished the night away, decked out in his miner's head-light so he could see a carp to club, or to make sure he didn't pee on his bait box.

Our waking patterns also differed, with me usually rising well before Brian, as I enjoyed the cool quiet of the morning. I would crawl out at first light to see a slight mist hovering over the river. The only movement, apart from the never-ending mass of water pushing by, were insects bobbing and bouncing around in the nearby reeds. There was usually not a cloud in the sky and the sun said "good-morning Wilson" by shooting slabs of warmth through the tree gaps until it reached a height where it could send a few rays directly at our tents.

For some reason I always checked our kayaks hadn't been taken in the middle of the night, although the chances of the 'Khancoban kayak stealers' finding us were slim. Then I would wait for the sun to drift up over the tree line to melt away the river mist. The odd fish would plop up, keeping a wary eye out for Brian, not that he needed to worry, with Brian asleep in his tent – a fact confirmed by the dulcet snoring tones wafting out through the gap in his tent flap.

Such was my most pleasant introduction to kayaking, and by the fifth day we drifted into Tintaldra, having covered some

100 kilometres. 'Tintaldra' is aboriginal for a 'young man by the water', which may be in honour of a Charles Huon de Kerilleau who was shown the area in 1837 by a group of young aborigines. Charles was the son of a French Royal who had fled France. Charles didn't hang around the area too long, possibly because back in 1837 there was no patisserie or baguette shop to keep him there.

Thirty or so years later a Mr. Sydney Grandison Watson commissioned the Tintaldra Store to be built where it still stands today, a fine example of old-time axe hacking, built mostly from River Red Gum and Red Stringy Bark Slabs. Ever the developer, this fellow Watson then had a hotel built which no longer exists. The present Hotel structure was built by 1874 and was originally known as the 'Pet Lamb', a far classier name for a pub than the Tintaldra Hotel. Nearby a punt used to ferry people and livestock across the Murray until 1892 when they built a bridge, which made it far easier to move 100 head of cattle across the river, seeing as only 10 at a time could fit on the punt. The town was a customs collection point until 1901 – but Tintaldra had seen better days - today it looks like only a few dozen people live there.

We were in the old 'Pet Lamb' as soon as we had put up our tents, showered and Brian had changed into his finest outfit. We were alone in the bar except for one old coot, perched up on a bar stool mesmerised by the bubbles rising in his beer.

"Hi guys," said the barman. "Welcome to the first pub on the Murray."

"I thought the Alpine Inn at Khancoban was the first pub on the Murray," I replied.

"Crap. Khancoban is not even on the bloody Murray. Everyone knows that. By the way, what are you travelling on?"

"Dagger Edisto," I replied.

"Good equipment?" he asked.

"Excellent. Travel well, stable and lots of room for our gear."

"Never heard of them. They must be quiet too as I did not hear you pull up."

"Eh?"

"Get dozens of riders through here. Had our fifteen year celebration a couple of years ago and we had dozens of them stay out the back. They were mainly on Harleys and Triumphs but some Ducati's. A few Hells Angels, Gypsy Jokers, Coffin Cheaters, and Bandidos. Only ten fights over the weekend so it was pretty quiet."

"Eh?" I said again.

Brian tapped me on the shoulder and quietly said to me, "You've run your race with this guy. He thinks we are on motor bikes, so let me do the talking from now on."

He turned to the barman. "A sight for sore eyes this pub, a great place."

"Thanks mate," he replied. "Alf's the name."

"And the pub Alf; been here long?"

"Been here for over a hundred years, mate. Now we are famous as the spot for bikers to stop at. Me and the missus love 'em."

Alf presumably meant the pub had been there over two hundred years, not he and his missus. Brian turned and whispered to me, "This is how you win over a local McOrist. A bit of charm goes a long way."

We weren't just here for the beer but to sample 'the best steaks in Victoria' so Brian asked Alf: "What time does the counter meal come on?"

Alf replied: "No meals tonight mate, it's Sunday. We don't do meals on a Sunday."

Chapter 5: 'in dripping clothes'

[We meet mosquitoes, and rain. We replenish supplies at the Walwa General Store, midway between Tintaldra and Jingellic.]

Rain

Apart from missing out on slab of steak for our evening meal, life was good. I had made it through the first tiny leg of our journey, a whole 100 kilometres of the 2500 and only 2400 to go.

Our next port of call would be Jingellic, passing through the township of Walwa on the way – 50 or so kilometres by the river - Brian thought it should only take us two days of paddling. By early afternoon we were away, after dropping Brian's car at Jingellic - we had only been off the river for a day, but I felt like I had come back home.

It was most pleasant as we were far from any road to hear car engine noises, there were no houses to bother us as we were cocooned in by trees and bushes and all we could hear were bird whistles and the smack of our paddles on the water. It was serenity, the real deal. Once more it was warm and sunny and we simply drifted along at the speed of the river, paddling a little and singing the odd children's nursery rhyme to entertain the cows. At about four Brian spotted a place to camp for the night – he had a choice of a myriad of pretty-pretty camping spots.

Now unsurprisingly his fishing bag of tricks failed once more, and I thought of mentioning to him that he might have the wrong bait or the wrong lure or his technique may be lacking, but I thought it best to say nothing. It was early days, and I still had great faith in his fishing prowess.

Not only the fishing gods but also the weather gods turned against us on the next afternoon. We set up camp early in a slight drizzle, which continued while we sat around the fire. My padding partner was not a happy man. For starters it was too wet to fish, but Brian also hated the rain because it brought out mosquitoes. He had on his long pants, a long-sleeved top, a hat, a mosquito net and was layered up in multi-coats of repellent, sitting in the middle of the smoke from the fire (in spite of it being the middle of summer) whacking away at mosquitoes like a semaphoring sailor.

Mosquitoes have been around for a long time. Back in 1770 the ship the 'Endeavour' was holed on the Great Barrier Reef, and the men had to camp close to the banks of a river on the shore. Joseph Banks wrote they too had to sit in the smoke from the fire:

the mosquitoes, whose peaceful dominions it seems we had invaded, spared no pains to molest as much as was in their power; they followed us into the smoke.

The rain seemed to tumble down relentlessly all night but it had become a consistent and irritating drizzle by the next morning. I managed to find some dry kindling by scraping away the outside wet bark on a stringy-bark gum tree. This dry bark with a few sheets of unused toilet paper had the fire going - Bear Grylls eat your heart out! The wet twigs on the dry bark smouldered for a while, and then the wet branches on them smouldered, leading to the wet logs on top of the branches smouldering too. By this time I had a plume of black smoke a hundred feet high, no doubt producing more carbon footprints than a coal fired electricity plant, but finally the little twigs flickered into flames and fire appeared.

It was not long before I had a real fire. The wet twigs on top of the dry bark dried out and burnt the small branches which dried and burnt the wet logs so I threw more logs on and soon I had a gigantic bonfire burning with red embers being thrown high up in the air. I could not get within fifty metres of it, but it dried me, my clothes and scorched everything in a twenty metre radius.

"Everything under control over there?" Brian yelled out, feeling the warmth from the blaze over by his fishing spot 200 metres away.

Not that Brian and Banks were alone in their dislike of mosquitoes, On more than one occasion Hovell tells us they *were utterly unable to obtain any rest, in consequence of the incessant and distressing attacks'*.

Cool paddling

By mid-morning we had packed up our wet gear and were on the river, now the colour of a grey thundercloud. I paddled hard to keep warm which kept me level with Brian and fortunately the rain stayed up in the clouds as we cruised along together. The river was now quite wide, 30 metres or more, and slow moving. I had dried out my clothes with the bonfire but I soon became wet and cold again from the paddle drips; unlike yesterday when the sun the drips had worked a treat to keep me cool, but now I couldn't find any control button to switch from cool to heat – my only solution was to keep paddling, to stop myself freezing.

Unfortunately, the rain started again and the wind continued so paddling wasn't the idyllic experience it had been for the past few days. My waterproof was not cut out for a kayaker, but better suited to a person huddling in the rain at the football, protecting their meat pie and can of beer from the rain. Oh, I thought, what I would do for a hot meat pie. The waterproof was far too loose so when I met a head wind it billowed out from under my arms and created a sail effect, slowing me down. I would pull, pull, pull then look left or right to see how far I had travelled, by measuring against a tree or landmark, then pull, pull, pull again, then check my bearings to find I was still level with the same tree. Holy Cow! I had not moved at all!

"How are you doing old son?" said Brian, who had stopped to wait for me.

"Some of us are born with natural upper body strength," I said to him. "I feel like a man of straw. You have the upper body strength of a gorilla but I think I have my strength distributed equally around my body. If we were bike riding across Europe, stopping at pubs, and eating fine food beside a warm open fire, and sipping buckets of the best German beer and being waited on by two buxom wenches who wanted our bodies to …"

He interrupted me. "Hold it there McOrist. Are you losing it? Are you cracking up?"

In 1830 Sturt and his men sometimes found it far better to be pulling on an oar than sitting still in the boat. Sturt wrote:

… the river had evidently fallen more than a foot, and was so shallow in several places, that we were obliged to haul the boat over them. On these occasions we were necessarily obliged to get out of her into the water, and had afterwards to sit still and to allow the sun to dry our clothes upon us.

The unemployed consequently envied those at the oars, as they sat shivering in their dripping clothes.

The Walwa General Store

An hour or so later we were inside a warm cabin at the Walwa camping ground. After a few days on the river the cabin was a palace by comparison, complete with hot water, a shower, a TV and a couple of bunks. I looked under the bunks for a left-behind raincoat and in the cupboards for a spare pillow that might not be missed.

The next day dawned warm and sunny so we decided to stay on an extra day to dry out. While I waited for my buddy to peg up his bags of laundry, I wrote down some items I felt may be needed the next time we kayaked.

First of all: a map of the river would be practical. It would show me where we were and how far we had to go to the next town and it needed to be in plastic covers as it would get wet. Then a song book would come in handy at times as singing would help me pass the time and keep the cows amused. We had tried singing a couple of songs we both thought we knew off by heart but could not remember more than the chorus. Happy Birthday was as good as it got. We would need a book each, in big print.

Finally, once the spick and span man had finished pegging clothes and was clad in his top-notch shirt and shorts (colour coordinated of course), we enjoyed what civilisation had to offer us at the Walwa General Store; a coffee from their cafe section, fuel for my car from their service centre, more kayaking food from the groceries department, new camping chairs in the camping goods department, and a couple of hamburgers from the take-away section, also part of the same Walwa General Store. It was a great little store.

(Well may you ask why we needed new camping chairs? The pocket-sized, light as a feather chairs I had bought, as a present for my kayaking cohort and me, turned out to be children's camping chairs. They broke into pieces as soon as we pushed down on the arms to stand up.)

We read, in the delightfully named 'Walwa World Community Newsletter', an article on two people doing a mammoth 30 minute cycle ride every morning, and because of this the local Shire would be asked to provide (and I quote): 'signage for cyclists and pedestrians as well as for kangaroos and wombats'. If my kayak had broken down at Walwa I would still be there today, cycling daily with the locals and watching the wombats and kangaroos read the road signs.

I'm not the only one to have a soft spot for Walwa. Way back in the 1850s an Irishman named Joseph Hanna (no doubt simply Joe to his mates) liked the area so much he even spent a few years digging ditches, with a shovel, to drain the swamps so he could plant an orchard. His fruit trees were free from any pests because he used to spray the fruit with a nicotine - tobacco mixture, which certainly knocked the fruit fly to the ground. What is did for lung cancer for those who ate Joe's fruit I have no idea.

Chapter 6: 'solitude and restfulness'

[Our method of leap-frogging the cars is explained. We enjoy our last days on a tranquil river, stopping when we reach Lake Hume. Brian and I part ways, intending to continue on in 12 months time.]

Mr Darcy

We, or should I say Brian, decided that the next leg would be our last hop for this year as it was only another hundred kilometres or so on the river, by which point we would be well onto Lake Hume, which we could paddle across to the weir at Albury. Brian suggested we shouldn't attempt to kayak all the way across the lake - it could be dangerous when the winds get up. His alternative was that we drop one car soon after the river runs into the lake and finish there, about 10 or 15 kilometres short of Albury.

I put my arm around his shoulders. "Are you suggesting we don't really kayak the whole river? Are you suggesting we skip the last 10 kilometres of Lake Hume and start again after the weir?"

"Yep, that is exactly what I am suggesting. If you would like to kayak all the way across the lake on your own, that's fine by me, I will wait for you at the weir. There is a little town right next to the weir called Bellbridge – you'll find me in the pub."

He went on: "And if they find your overturned kayak and no remains of you except your straw hat I will personally drive to Coffs Harbour and explain to Suzanne what a dickhead you were thinking it was safe to row across Lake Hume against my sound advice. I will stay with her for a while, as I know she has a secret pining for me, a passionate one I believe. I will console her in her grief, and most likely woo her with affection and love-making so she never need think of you again. I will be her Mr Darcy.'

I just shook my head, saying: "Mr Bean more likely."

We drove out of Walwa towards Albury following the river down looking for a place where we could leave one of the cars by Lake Hume. Just in case it is not 100% clear what this car-leapfrogging meant, the following diagram explains how we were to get from Point A to Point B.

- On the first line you see both cars and kayaks going to the end, Point B.
- On the second line one car takes both kayaks back to the start, Point A.
- On the third line you see both kayaks paddling on the river down to the end (Point B).
- On the fourth line the one car at the end, with both kayaks on board, goes back to the start (Point A) to pick up the other car.
- The last line shows both cars going down to the end, which then becomes a new point A to repeat the process for the next hop.

We drove through Burrowye, Thologolong (try saying that with a mouthful of jelly beans) and Bungil. These places consisted of no more than a couple of falling down farm houses, with either a few barnyard fowls scratching around or a slinky-looking sheep dog sleeping on the porch.

For all we knew one of these gone-to-seed farm houses could have been the homestead of the first white female settler up this way, a certain Miss Murphy. Back in the early 1800s an English gentleman, as they all were back in the early 1800s I am sure, by the name of Robert Mason landed in Sydney in 1827, took a few odd jobs, from being a policeman to steering a boat on the Parramatta River - the main tributary of Sydney Harbour - then working on farms before he finally bought into a piece of dirt on the Upper Murray called Biggerie Station. Before he headed off he married a Miss Murphy, of Parramatta way, and this lassie became the first white woman that went to live on the Upper Murray. She had a ball by all accounts, getting groceries and other requirements from Sydney when her husband made the trip once a year with his bullock wagon, a three month journey, and she joined in with early settlers life of tanning the leather needed for a new set of boots, helping in the fields by slashing away at the crops with a scythe, and then grounding the wheat for flour with a hand mill before she could whip up some pumpkin scones. Ah, the good old days. They even produced a wee bonnie lad in 1838 and he was the first white child born in this neck of the woods.

Taking both our cars Brian and I reached the start of Lake Hume and soon after we found a track down to the lake where, as luck would have it, we bumped into a couple of families camping there. They were more than happy to look after one of our cars for a few days. We gave them a wave after leaving Brian's car by a tree near their tents hoping to see them again in a few days, but more so Brian's car, unless they were car-wreckers on their annual holiday. In that case, Brian's car would soon be in pieces and sold around a myriad of car wrecker yards.

The next morning we were back on the river, chatting away and telling each other how much we loved the solitude and serenity of the river. I felt like Dr Frederick Cook who, when surrounded by icebergs on a voyage to Antarctica a hundred years ago, in the good ship 'Belgica', wrote: *'there is a solitude and restfulness about the whole scene which can only be felt; it cannot be described'.*

That evening the nearby families of fish chatted away happily to each other, ignoring whatever bait the master fisherman tossed at them. I vaguely remember falling into bed at something like seven o'clock, leaving Brian staring at the campfire, telling himself fishing tales.

Approaching Lake Hume (Albury)

One glorious day followed another, with the morning sunlight shooting through the trees as the river silently passed by our camp site; now a tranquil stream about 40 metres wide, with its riverside reeds and bushes brimming with zippy insects in the first hours of the day.

We were soon within a day of Lake Hume, but we could still see and feel a gentle current as we went around the smooth pebble stone corners. We had enough current to keep us moving down the seemingly motionless straight stretches of the river, with only minimal paddling effort. We plodded and drifted our way along, always looking out for something interesting to help pass the time, something like a cow.

You may be getting the impression that there was naught all to communicate with apart from cows, ducks, one lonely baby snake bobbing its way across the river, parrots, magpies, the occasional swan, bell-birds and early morning kookaburras, and you would be right. People were in short supply. There was virtually no one else on the river except for the once-in-a-while old coot in his tinnie, parked under a shady tree, fast asleep, fishing rod in hand, enjoying a day without his wife.

We felt we were on Australia's number one river, at its most sublime. There were just gnarled old gum trees, weeping willows and riverside reeds, each of them reflected in the restful mirror-like river. We would swing round a bend expecting to meet someone or see something different, but no, still more twisted and wrinkled gum trees, weeping willows and reeds and yet another bend ahead. We would drift around that bend and ahead would be another bend, sometimes with the grassy paddocks of the farmland coming right down to the river where another family of cows would be waiting for us to go by, cheering wildly like we were the peloton in the Tour de France.

We did not part company, except for 100 metres or so when Brian decided to race a duck or sprint to a corner for some exercise, two activities with which I refused to get involved. Usually we travelled along together, as good friends would do.

We lounged the early night hours away by our flickering campfire, in our camp chairs, watching the stars of south-east Australia float along overhead. The only person watching us was the man in the moon who looked mighty handsome and even half holy as he peeped at us from behind a cloud.

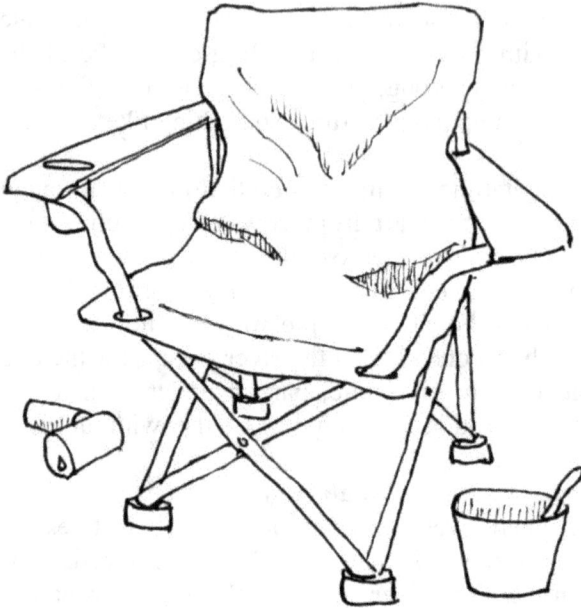

Sturt, Hume and Hovell rarely waxed lyrical about their travels, but on one occasion Sturt wrote, at a spot near the Murrumbidgee River:

From a small hill that lay to our left Mr. M'Leay and I enjoyed a most beautiful view. Beneath us to the S. E. the rich and lightly timbered valley through which the Morumbidgee flows, extended, and parts of the river were visible through the dark masses of swamp-oak by which it was lined, or glittering among the flooded-gum trees, that grew in its vicinity.

Likewise with Hovell; his journals usually contained only the most basic of facts, and accounts of the hardships they faced, but when he and Hume reached southern Victoria he was struck by the scenery:

Tuesday, 14th December. Never did I behold a more charming and gratifying sight, at least not where it is in its natural state. I have travelled from Launceston to Hobart Town, but in the whole distance, I do not recollect seeing any one place where it can at all be compared with the spot we have passed and this before us.

The end of stage 1

For a couple of modern day guys, it was suddenly all over; too soon. Early one afternoon we coasted around yet another corner of small shiny pebbles and we were onto Lake Hume, and bugger me not long after we saw the two families, and surprisingly Brian's car was still nearby, even more surprisingly with all its wheels. We beached the kayaks, clamoured out and shook hands. We had made it to the end of stage 1, Albury. Well, Brian and I knew very well it was a few kilometres short of Albury, but no one else would ever know. We had done close to 350 kilometres; only 2200 to reach the end of the Murray.

With a wave to the car wrecker families, a wave to the Murray and a wave to all its fish - population largely undiminished from 10 days ago may I point out - we went back to Walwa to pick up my car. Then it was a 1000 kilometre drive back home to Coffs Harbour for me, and a 30 kilometre drive back to Barnawatha for Brian.

"Finish it next year?" were Brian's farewell words.

We had stopped very near to the place where Hume and Hovell must have first crossed the Murray River, on Nov 20 1824. They, like us, enjoyed the scenery and the general appearance of the country, hearing the bell-birds ringing merrily. They had seen the Murray a few days earlier downstream from here but the two lads were unable to work out how to cross the river

69

because of the lagoons and swamps, so at first they went downstream near where Albury is today where Hovell tells us they both hacked their names into a couple of trees: '*in the solid wood of a healthy tree I cut my name, Hovell, Novr. 17/24*'.

They continued further downstream, hoping to discover a ford they could wade over to the southern side but without success, finding that the river became even wider or, '*of somewhat increased magnitude*', to use Hovell's words. They could not find a crossing place so they turned around and went back upstream still in search for a suitable spot and it was a couple of days later they were at a point close to where Brian and I now stood. Hume and Hovell then built a boat to cross over to the southern Victorian side of the Murray. Hovell wrote:

Saturday, 20th November... We then put the tarpaulin over the frame, as we had before done by the cart. At 11 o'clock we began to send the articles across, and by 4 p.m. horses, bullocks, etc., etc., were over, but it was nearly with the loss of Mr. Hume's bullock.

STAGE 2:

2007. Another two weeks on the river

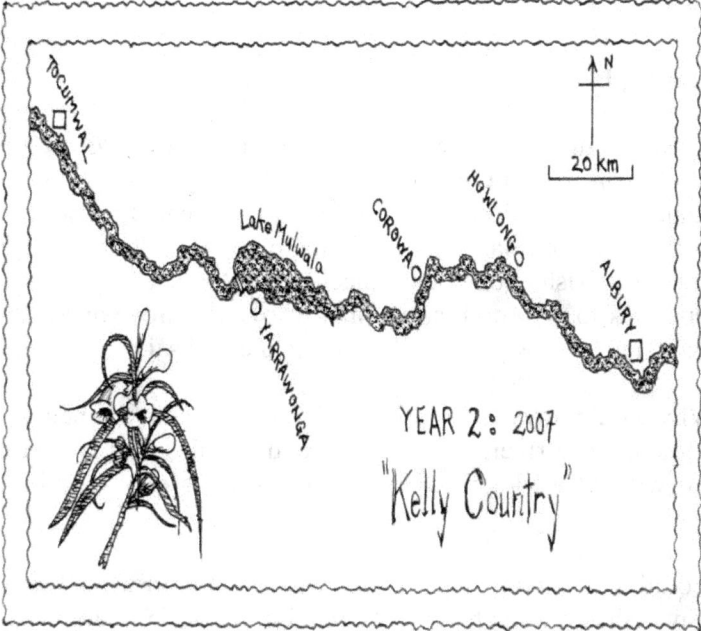

Map showing the river from TOCUMWAL through Lake Mulwala, YARRAWONGA, COROWA, HOWLONG to ALBURY. Scale 20 km. YEAR 2: 2007 "Kelly Country"

Chapter 7: 'the blood flows'

[We meet at Albury 12 months later and put in just below the Hume Weir. Brian has a wonderful present for me. He tries to expand my mind in relation to the sights along the river, with little success. We eat well. Brian keeps the wild-life awake at night.]

Brian's plans

A year went by and we ignored each other, as good men friends can do, but in late January 2007 we were together again, at Brian's place in the Indigo Valley, near Barnawatha in North East Victoria, just 30 kilometres from Albury. As his good lady Trish cooked us a succulent last supper my thoughts went back to my good lady's final words as I drove away from Coffs Harbour, two days before. Suzanne had said:

"Why would anyone choose to drive a thousand kilometres, to paddle down a river, eating muesli and noodles for two weeks? And without a fridge within easy reach for a cool beer in the evenings? "

I could still picture her in the rear-vision mirror as I drove away - shaking her head and probably muttering "crazy-as-a-loon". She certainly had little time for these words:

Of the gladdest moments in human life methinks, is the departure upon a distant journey into unknown lands. The blood flows with the fast circulation of childhood. Excitement lends unwonted vigour to the muscle.

Which are the thoughts of Richard Burton; not the film actor, a different Burton. This one wandered across to Mecca a hundred and fifty years ago, disguised as an Arab and he also stumbled around the centre of Africa looking for the source of the Nile.

Brian's thoughts were not quite so eloquent but he did state that our next 'stepping-stone' should be from Albury down to Tocumwal passing through many a small town on the way. The trip would be another 350 river kilometres as once again we only had two weeks available – we did work occasionally. Brian had kayaked parts of the river before and assured me it was all child's play, a piece of cake, plain sailing. I hoped so.

"Magic Murray country here old cock," he proudly explained. "The river will be magic too. Big river red gums, great camping spots, clean water, still a good river current and oodles of fish for me to catch." I thought he may have said noodles not oodles but I let it slide.

He then lent towards me and said, quietly, that for most of the next three hundred kilometres on the river we would only be an hour or so drive away from his home, so his darling wife Trish would doubtless pop down with a picnic lunch for us on some days, which meant our lunch breaks may be longer than they were last year. However, just in case she forgot we should buy some stocks of unleavened bread and cheese.

He then told me about his friends - the Gibbs who owned the Barnawatha pub – partners with him in a small vineyard. They, like Brian, loved the finer elements of food and drink so we could expect them to meet us for an evening meal one night and they would bring along a bar-b-que, a couple of rib-eye steaks, bottles of French red and even some lemon soufflés for dessert.

So, it was becoming a little clearer that some of our hardships, such as being forced to eat rib-eye steaks and drink French wine, were not quite as arduous as those experienced by the explorers of the early 1800s. Hovell tells us that after reaching the southern coast, they ate one of their bullocks (named Captain):

Sunday, 19th December. Here we stopped to kill a bullock, which we found impossible to take any further. Poor old

"Captain" had been our leader the whole distance coming ... the men had now been without meat one week, and had had only one kangaroo for a fortnight ... they were becoming very weak.

It was fortunate for the men that I killed the bullock, as there are not more than two that have shoes to their feet. Therefore the skin comes in for mocassins for them, which answer the place of shoes.

(I doubted that Brian and I would be skinning a bullock, or any other animal, to make ourselves a set of moccasins.)

We meet another old-time explorer

A few kilometres downstream from Albury we would be waving goodbye to Hume and Hovell - they had travelled down river from where Albury is today, looking for a place to cross the Murray, before heading back upstream. But later on we would be meeting up with Major Thomas Mitchell, another 1800s explorer. Mitchell crossed the Murray where Howlong is now located, back in 1836. He was a Scot, and an Army man, who managed to reach the exulted rank of Lieutenant Colonel (way ahead in rank to our Captain Sturt) but most importantly he became the Surveyor General for NSW in 1828. This meant he could place himself up near the front of the explorers queue and of his four expeditions his third is of greatest interest to a Murray River tragic. Mitchell was a little like Sturt, traipsing around the countryside and generally following rivers to see where they ended up, but Mitchell generally clip-clopped alongside rivers – horse and bullocks hauling carts were his forte - none of this boating stuff that Brian, Sturt and I were into.

On one of his sojourns, Mitchell distributed to each of his men a suit of new clothing; consisting of grey trousers and '*a red woollen shirt, the latter article, when crossed by white braces, giving the men somewhat of a military appearance.*'

(If only I had a red woollen shirt, with braces, to give me a military appearance, Brian would have liked that.)

Anyway, on this third adventure, in 1836, Mitchell followed the course of the Murrumbidgee River down to where it met the Murray River and he then followed the Murray, at first downstream, exploring the section between the Murrumbidgee and the Darling River. He had a look around there but then called out "Whoa! Go back!" to his horse, and he and his men turned around and followed the Murray back upstream.

Mitchell stayed close to the Murray, following it all the way past where Swan Hill sits today before leaving it and turning south to see a little of the Victorian countryside before he headed back to Sydney, crossing the Murray near where Howlong now sits, but not stopping long. I presume he was in a hurry for the same reason as Hume and Hovell; for a hot bath in Sydney.

Mitchell was a man capable of writing up an excellent journal and he was especially fascinated by a corroboree (calling it a corrobory):

The dance always takes place at night, by the light of blazing boughs, and to time beaten on stretched skins, accompanied by a song. The dancers paint themselves white, and in such remarkably varied ways that no two individuals are at all alike.

There can be little doubt that the corrobory is the medium through which the delights of poetry are enjoyed, in a limited degree, even by these primitive savages of New Holland.

Serenity once again

The next morning Trish blew kisses to us as we departed, warning me to be understanding of Brian's snoring as he was having more sinus problems. She was no doubt looking forward to two weeks of peace and quiet at home while the man of her life (Brian) was away with his old chum (me). By early afternoon we were on the river, pushing off just below the weir at Albury. Brian was grinning from ear to ear: he was a happy-chappy; back on his river and no doubt looking forward to tonight's fishing, not to mention the next 10 days of fishing.

The current bowled along at a lively pace just below the Hume Weir so I thought we would make Tocumwal in a week but Brian could see us managing thirty kilometres a day at best and he was sure it would take us two weeks, especially when he noticed I still had my old plastic paddle.

We pushed off, juggled our butts to get comfortable, touched the foot pedals to make sure they worked okay (none of this 'check your boat properly before setting off' routine for us) and rolled the arms over to see if the paddling stoke still worked. The weir water pushed us along gently and it all came back to me - left arm forward, a twist of the wrist, the plop of the paddle in the water on the left side, a pull on the water, and then the right arm went forward. Pleasurable paddling it was, just like last year.

I then noticed a blue sign on a tree, with the number 2220, in white.

"What is that number?" I asked.

"How far to go."

"What?"

"How far to go. The 2220 sign means that there are 2220 kilometres to the end of the river, the Murray mouth as it is called, where the Murray meets the sea. There will be these blue distance markers all the way now, usually stuck up high on an old red gum on the bank. They are placed at two kilometre intervals along the entire length of the river so the next one we see will be 2218."

I put down my paddle and clapped my hands together a few times. "Well bugger me. I like that. It will give me something to look forward to."

The current speed lost a little momentum not long after leaving the weir, but we paddled away enthusiastically. It was Day 1 and we skimmed along past the outskirts of Albury, under the Melbourne to Sydney railway line, under the Hume Highway linking Wodonga and Albury and then into the quiet countryside. From then I moved into a gentler paddling mode.

At our first rest spot Brian, bless his little heart, gave me a book of maps of the river, 'River Murray Charts'. These maps were just what I needed; they showed the river in minute detail all the way from Albury to Renmark in South Australia, each map page covering only 40 or so kilometres of the river. They even included the blue distance marker signs and other good to know information like camping sites, creek names, and national park areas, and even some not-so-essential information to a kayaker, like 'mud banks', 'burnt tree', 'high rock shelf' and 'keep close to the sand in low water'. I thanked my paddling partner for his gift.

The river below Albury was different to the 'Upper Murray' we were on last year. Up Tintaldra way it felt like a stream weaving its way down a valley but now it was a river, a wide river, slowly moving its way through flat farming land, the banks lined with grass, reeds or willows to the water's edge; the willows leaning well into the water at times, depending on the bend of the river. Soon after leaving the outskirts of Albury we started to see a succession of lagoons on each side, extending away for what seemed like a few kilometres at times; formed by the winding of the river. Mum and dad ducks with the kids trailing were everywhere and we even saw the occasional pair of gliding swans. The land in between the river and the lagoons consisted of swamps and ground which looked decidedly slushy, often with clumps of large gums, overgrown with vines and no doubt swarming with masses of red-bellied black snakes.

We noticed a creek coming in from our left (the Wodonga Creek), and then more lagoons off to our right (Horseshoe Lagoon). Courtesy of Brian's 'River Murray Charts' map book - I now knew exactly where we were, and what lay ahead.

As was mentioned last year, Hume and Hovell first bumped into the Murray a little upstream from where we were, and they then ventured down this way, on the northern side of the Murray, as they looked for a place to cross. From Hovell's description the river has not changed:

... we found that to keep along its banks was impossible, as the lagoons and swamps in most places completely shut us out, some of them forming a half circle, the centre part extending to a distance of two miles and the two ends coming to this river.

Many of these creeks are as wide as the river itself, therefore we only got to the river in two places until we got to the distance of about eight or nine miles.

He was impressed with the river, the countryside and the wildlife:

Here the river appeared to us as it did when we first saw it, but if at all different, it is with a more majestic appearance,

The country all around us has a very fine appearance. In some places there is not more than half a dozen trees in a hundred acres. The swamps and creeks ... are full of fish and wild ducks. We also saw two black swans on one of the creeks, being the first we have seen since leaving home.

(We and the Murray River now bid a fond farewell to Hume and Hovell. After finding their crossing place upstream, they headed off down south, and they saw no more of the Murray, except for when they crossed it (at the same place), on their return trip to Sydney.)

A Harley man

It was Day 1 and I retired early, with a meal of two-minute pasta inside me and a cosy sleeping bag around me. It was heaven. Ah! I had forgotten the joy of sleeping in a tent, breathing in all that wonderful fresh country night air, and listening to the absolute silence of the countryside at night. It was pitch black and pin-drop quiet. There were no cars honking. No TV sets blaring. No neighbours abusing or bonking. It was bliss. Deep sleep came without effort.

My deep sleep was shattered an hour later. Some bastard in a Harley Davidson had pulled up right next to my tent, revving the guts out of his Harley engine. And this Marlon Brando wannabe kept revving it up, again, again, again and again.

But there was no bike, only Brian snoring. It was like gunfire, or even a machine gun, full-throated and guttural, loud and continuous, going full blast. Trish was right, he was having sinus problems. No one else within a ten-mile radius seemed to be disturbed by this, but after an hour of snore-listening I was still wide awake, as taut as a sling shot band. Then I remembered a book *Relief Without Drugs* by an Ainslie Meares which I had read many years ago. Good old Ainslie had a wonderful relaxation method and to help insomnia - start with relaxing your hands and feet and then move onto relaxing your arms, legs then the upper body and face.

I tried but I could still hear the volley and thunder from Brian's machine gun mouth. 'Be patient' I told myself, try again; but still I could hear the Bren gun.

"Hey Brian," I whispered. "Can you roll over? You're snoring."

His only response was to keep snoring.

"Hey Brian," I said a little more loudly. "Can you roll over? You're snoring."

His snoring continued.

"Brian," I yelled. "Hey, hey, hey. Roll over. Roll over"

And the snoring went on.

I then screamed at the top of my voice. "Brian! Wake up. Wake up! WAKE UP."

From the other side of the river, from a farmhouse we did not even know was there, I heard a loud male voice yell back at me: "If you don't shut the fuck up, I'll come over there and punch your fucking head in."

I froze. But suddenly there was silence, real silence. Brian had even stopped snoring.

"What! What! What was that?" he muttered, before dozing off again. I then had a period of solitude for at least 30 seconds, before the Harley rumble interspersed with machine gun fire started up again.

So I started my relaxation process again but I could still hear the snoring, so enough was enough. I got up, pulled out my tents pegs and dragged my tent about 50 metres away from Brian's tent - moving was an easy solution - problem solved. I should have done it hours ago.

But those pearls of wisdom of my year 11 Science teacher at Yarrawonga High School came back to haunt me: "Now young McOrist, don't ever forget that sound travels better at night because of the cooler air temperature." Big deal I thought then, but that old teacher was on the button. As clear as a bell from 50 metres away I could still hear the sound of a Harley gurgling up from the throat of my kayaking partner. So, you guessed it, I got up again to drag the tent a further 50 metres away.

Now I ask you, why does the ear strain to hear the faintest sound of snoring? Why didn't Crick and Watson solve that little puzzle instead of knocking down copious pints at "The Eagle" public house in Cambridge, while formulating an accurate description of DNA - the genetic instructions for the so called Blueprint of Life? But in a scientific discovery ranking up with Crick and his chum Watson I found a solution to the problem - move another 50 metres away, behind a large gum tree to block out the sound completely.

I was finally asleep by six o'clock, but woken at seven by someone calling out: "Cooee. Cooee." It was Brian, wandering around looking for me. I heard him again: "Cooee. Has anyone seen an unshaven scruff of a man wearing a faded blue truckies singlet and old football shorts? Cooee."

Short Cuts

Day 2, and by mid morning we were away, quickly slipping into our kayaking groove, paddling along together or separately when Brian felt the need for some harder pulling, stopping on the hour for a rest and a body stretch, as we had the previous year, and then paddling on. It was highly enjoyable. I saw the 2188 blue marker sign drift by, or we drifted by it to be more precise, and I thought: "How ridiculous is that? We have 2188 kilometres to go to the end of the river." It was such a high number it meant naught to me.

There was one fundamental difference in how Brian and I handled the trip. For Brian, being somewhat knowledgeable with regards to flora and fauna and of the river, he enjoyed the aesthetic aspects of the trip far more than I. He would love to see a fish skim by, or hear a bird hoot or holler.

"Did you see that Murray cod just back there?"

Or, "that bird call sounds like a Gilbert's Whistler. Did you hear it?"

Or, "see that huge '*Eucalyptus camaldulensis*' over there? What a beautiful river red gum. It must be over thirty metres high. What goes through your mind when you look at a tree as magnificent as that?"

To me it looked just like another gnarled old gum tree.

Not so to Brian. "That could be the home to those sulphur-crested cockatoos we saw just before. By the way, much later on we pass what is considered to be the biggest red gum in the world, a long way ahead yet, near Mildura I think. We must make sure we don't miss it."

As we know, carp did not win Brian. He put on his teaching hat to explain that some expert mind a hundred years ago decided to stock up fish dams here with them - a fish native to

Central Asia – and carp are now known as the rabbits of the river because they breed like rabbits and eat all they can. They were now the most common fish in the Murray, so I guess he had a lot of carp to hate. He particularly disliked the carp's habit of stirring up the water and mud by the edge of the river – where they inhale sediment and sift it through their gills – a process called 'mumbling'.

"Sort of like hearing your wife nag at you," he said, "letting it all pass through your ears and out the other side."

Because of their 'mumbling' in the shallows Brian could spot one from 100 metres. He would glide quietly up and try to whack it with his paddle, crying out "Take that you bastard!", an activity he never tired of, but I doubt he took out more than a couple of carp. While Brian concentrated on thrashing away at the odd carp, or embarking on an imaginary whistling conversation with a bird as he tried to mimic their warble, or most commonly commenting on how close a gnarled old gum tree resembled parts of the female anatomy, I concentrated on where we were, and how far it might be before we stopped for a rest.

Brian had been down this part of the river before and told me not to worry if he suddenly disappeared into a bunch of reeds or willows to check out a possible short-cut - the river looped back on itself continually. Many a time I would sit and wait for him as he disappeared into a bunch of two metre high reeds – they often lined the banks of the river on both sides and waved at us, like swaying streamers - expecting never to see him again. But no, after anywhere between two minutes and an hour he would burst back out of the reeds and tell me to follow him. I joined him as instructed, and we would then meander through a lagoon together, me blindly tagging along 10 metres behind, ever watchful for red-bellied black snakes lying in wait on the logs we slid past.

I had no option but to quietly accept the fact that for next couple of hours I would be paddling through algae and weed filled lagoons, reeds to my left, reeds to my right, saying hello to ducks and other water birds who rarely ever saw a white man, let alone two white men in a kayaks, wandering through their private water hole. Sometimes we lost time and paddled more because we would meet reeds that we couldn't pull through or too many fallen trees that would stop our path so we had to turn around and slog it back to the main river.

The trees in the lagoons were often dead, leafless and sapless, but battling our way through in a kayak did have a certain thrill about it, certainly much more than a thrill than if we were higher up in a boat. In the kayaks we were right down in the water and our eyes were only a metre above the water level. We were so close to the vegetation in the water that we could touch the reeds as we skimmed through, push ourselves away from fallen logs that blocked our path, drag the kayaks through shallow water and pull ourselves by hand through shallow algae covered ponds.

An aspect of kayaking that won me over was how quietly we travelled. We could glide to within cherry stone spitting distance of animals; kangaroos by the side of the river, ducks in the water, cormorants in the shallows and even red-bellied black snakes snoozing on a log, if they had been there. (We did not see a snake of any description but I felt them watching me.)

And then as if by magic, we would burst out of the lagoon, and be back onto the river a little further downstream.

Wake Up Call

"Canoe tree!" yelled Brian at one stage as he floated across to the bank. We both hopped out and stared at an old red gum tree with a huge canoe shape carved out of the bark, about three metres long and a metre wide. Canoes were the first method of river transport for the aborigines. They would make an outline of the shape with a cutting stone and then cut more deeply into the tree, prying the bark off in one piece. I was highly impressed with the canoe tree, or at least quite impressed with the canoe shape. Obviously I walked around the area expecting to pick up a few old didgeridoos, boomerangs, spears and shields and of course I found nothing except a few ants' nests.

We saw no other 'native' sights that day or the next but it didn't matter as the days were idyllic - cool weather, no wind and red gum after red gum lining the side of the river, 20, 30 even 40 metre high with gnarled trunks and twisted branches taking in the sight of two blue kayaks passing by. We ambled along gently, stopping frequently in the morning and even more frequently in the afternoon until about four o'clock when Brian chose another crack-a-jack fishing hole to camp next to. Off he'd go fishing but without luck, with me rudely telling him that I quite liked fresh fish.

"It will happen my good man, mark my words," he said after a couple of evenings of me doubting his fishing skills, "and you will be sick of fish before this is all over. Now I have to make a phone call to my dear friends Michael and Sue Gibb as we are close now to Barnawatha where they live. As I mentioned, they said they would bring a meal down one night."

"Perhaps they can bring some fish?" I enquired.

86

We were in a routine, of sorts. I woke up as the sun rose, at cockcrow, not that we could hear a cock crowing; only cackling kookaburras having their morning chit-chat to each other.

Back in the 1800s Sturt got a kick out of the kookaburra's delight in waking people early in the morning. His turn of phrase: 'chorus of wild spirits', quite appealed to me:

... a laughing jackass (alcedo gigantea,) a species of king's-fisher, a singular bird, found in every part of Australia.

Its cry, which resembles a chorus of wild spirits, is apt to startle the traveller who may be in jeopardy, as if laughing and mocking at his misfortune. It is a harmless bird, and I seldom allowed them to be destroyed, as they were sure to rouse us with the earliest dawn.

Duck and pork, but no fish

The weather gods stayed with us as we had mild mornings, warm and sunny days with rolling clouds overhead and no wind at our water level. The river wound around and around, coming right back on itself at times. Sometimes we could even see the river off to our left or right after it had gone up to a sharp bend and then come back.

Mid-afternoon one day Brian told me: "In a couple more bends we'll be at a place called Creamery Road Reserve. I told Michael and Sue to meet us there. It is where the Indigo Creek meets the Murray."

By late afternoon we had our two tents up. Remembering the nightly nasal sound of my best buddy, this time my tent site was 100 metres away. When Brian's friends turned up their first words were to ask if we had a fight, seeing our tents so far apart.

"You don't want to know," said Brian. "Michael, Sue, I don't really want to do this but I have to introduce you to my kayaking friend. He may not look like a kayaker in his straw hat, blue singlet and board shorts, and the more I see of him in a kayak I doubt he will ever perform like one either."

Now, I thought these friends of Brian would bring along sausages for us to have on the open fire, or cook up a fish that Brian had caught; but far from it. For starters they offered us a glass of Eden Valley Riesling, or a Pinot Noir from Mornington, with a cheese platter of Milawa Blue, King Island Brie. Then they fed us on roasted vegetables, green salad and a range of great meats from a butcher in Wodonga. We had duck, pistachio sausages and Kastler pork, washed down with a stunning Barossa Shiraz. To make us sleep well we topped it all off with a glass or two of Rutherglen Muscat. I have nothing but good words for Sue and Michael.

88

Back in the 1800s Sturt had a few good words to say about a fishing method used by the aboriginals:

They would slip, feet foremost, into the water as they walked along the bank of the river, as if they had accidentally done so, but, in reality, to avoid the splash they would necessarily have made if they had plunged in head foremost.

As surely as they then disappeared under the surface of the water, so surely would they re-appear with a fish writhing upon the point of their short spears.

He compared the water skills of the aborigines to an otter, saying:

the very otter scarcely exceeds them in power over the finny race, and so true is the aim of these savages, even under water, that all the fish we procured from them were pierced either close behind the lateral fin, or in the very centre of the head.

(As a fisherman Brian cast from the shore; slipping feet first into the water to spear fish was not in his bag of tricks.)

Hovell also tells us of another aboriginal fishing method, which involved knocking the fish out using the sap in the bark of willow trees.

It appears they are caught in dams where there is a running stream, as there is one they have made now in front of us. They are driven into the dam by the natives at one end, which is closed up when they think they have got sufficient.

They are made intoxicated by the bark of the willow tree, which they throw on to the place. By this they are supposed to be brought to the top. The natives then get into the water and throw them out.

(Brian never thought of catching fish this easy way. He was a man who liked a challenge.)

By early afternoon the next day Brian and I were at Howlong, surrounded by various lagoons and anabranches that spread out from the Murray near the town.

There, in a move that surprised the both of us, we walked past passed the Howlong Hotel to find a more favourable spot, a cafe with seats outside, where we ate multiple pies and drank multiple coffees, passing rascally comments on the girls as they walked by, quietly to ourselves of course. If a girl ever looked vaguely in our direction, we focused firmly on the pie.

In his journal Sturt occasionally wrote on the fairer aboriginal sex, and not in a complimentary way, saying the '*loathsome condition and hideous countenances of the women would, I should imagine, have been a complete antidote to the sexual passion.*'

In a rather rash generalisation on aboriginal men he adds: '*like all savages, they consider their women as secondary object.*'

He relates how the men give food to their women by throwing food '*over their shoulders the bones they have already picked, with a nonchalance that is extremely amusing.*'

(Note: They are Sturt's words, not mine. And Brian and I rarely throw food to our wives, nonchalantly.)

Chapter 8: 'lofty yarra trees'

[The birds at Howlong say goodbye. Brian's 'find of the trip' at Corowa. We meet a noisy tradesman at Wagunyah.]

Fish Lift

Howlong to Yarrawonga, with its weir and Lake Mulwala, was to be our next little gallivant, one hundred kilometres by river. I could find no record that Mitchell or anyone of note crossed the Murray where Yarrawonga is today but it's a far more attractive place than Howlong, if you enjoy water-skiing or looking at dead red-gum trees. In the late 1930s the Yarrawonga Weir was built (largest of all the sixteen weirs or locks on the Murray River, I may add) and Lake Mulwala was formed, creating a water-skiers paradise, but killing off a few thousand gum trees in the process.

The Yarrawonga Weir raises the water level of the River Murray to allow flows into the irrigation channels under gravity, of huge interest to our farming friends, but it's the flow allowed down the Murray which is of more interest to Brian and his fellow fishermen - low water levels and poor water quality gets them a little peeved and they struggle to snare a Murray cod or a golden perch - known as yellowbelly in New South Wales and callop in South Australia. Of bigger interest to fishermen (and fish for that matter) is that the Yarrawonga Weir has a fish lift. Yes you read it correctly, a fish lift, built in 1994 to provide an opportunity for fish to travel upstream of the weir, something which has been a little difficult for them since the dam wall went up in 1939. The yellow-belly is a fish that likes to travel around and their movement has been restricted by weirs and other barriers so they may be the ones it's designed for.

At Yarrawonga I planned to see an old friend, Colin Charmstrom who lived on Lake Mulwala. Colin was always a friendly chap and said he would love to see us, telling me that his place was easy to find from the river as he had a pontoon boat moored outside. It was the only pontoon boat so we couldn't miss it.

Neither Brian nor I knew what a pontoon boat looked like, but we hoped to find it when we were back in Yarrawonga in a week's time.

Cockatoos

We were on the river at Howlong by four o'clock and we stopped for the night just 10 kilometres downstream. The foot pump bellows I used to blow up my air bed had developed a leak but Brian managed to plug it with some duct tape. He explained to me in great detail that duct tape was the most essential spare item one can bring on a kayaking trip, the second most essential item being someone like him who could plug a hole in an air pipe with duct tape. To be honest his duct taping skills did impress me, but I didn't shoot his praises; because men-friends just don't.

We had camped in cockatoo heaven – the cockatoo being a bird with the harshest-discordant-bird call of any bird known to man. An extraordinary large flock had selected a tree close to our camp site and they croaked out their raucous calls until the sun went down.

Well may the greenies of this world tell me the cockatoo screeching is to warn each other of predators, or to allow individuals to recognise one another, or tell the others if they are cranky, or keep the flock together, but if we had a gun we would have blasted a round or two in their direction.

They seemed to be telling each other, 'nice sunset, nice sunset, nice sunset'. We were both awake before sunrise as were the cockatoos, softly saying to each other: 'Nice sunrise, nice sunrise, nice sunrise…'

A number of the old-age explorers mentioned mentioned cockatoos - white parrots they were known as. William Dampier in 1688, was the first, then Sturt in the early 1800s commented on their animated way of talking and his men were not adverse to taking pot-shots at these birds.

… among the land birds the most noticeable were white parrots, which flew a great many together. (Dampier)

… the cockatoos we had alarmed when descending into the creek had a nest. These noisy birds kept incessantly screeching… made the valley reverberate with their harsh and discordant notes. (Sturt)

… a flight of cockatoos passed over their tents and one of his men 'with his usual anxiety, trying to get a shot at them'. (Sturt)

There is a second problem with cockatoos or galahs as they were known to Allan Cunningham, who lived in Sydney in the early 1800s and was employed as the 'Botanical Collector to his late Majesty'. He tells us the bird *'comes in from sunrise for about two hours, same in the evening for about two hours of sunset.'*

(Well Mr Cunningham, nothing has changed in a couple of hundred years. The blessed cockatoo still enjoys the first and last couple of hours each day for a hubbub and hoo-ha.)

In spite of the cockatoo, Mitchell thought highly of the Murray River at Howlong. In his words, the *'grass grew luxuriantly'* and the river's edge was dotted with *'the lofty yarra trees and the low verdant alluvial flats of the Murray.'*

(We will cross Mitchell's tracks again, further on down the Murray.)

A clothes line

I looked over the map book and noted the Corowa camping ground was only 30 kilometres away so we should get there in one day, which suited Brian because his good lady Trish would be meeting us there – it was his birthday.

By late afternoon we had made it, with its Victorian buddy town of Wagunyah over the river, just as the sun was dropping out of sight. We started to put up our tents when Brian yelled across at me, "Look at this! What a find! I have been looking for one of these for years."

He held up a piece of string with a hook at each end and I said, "You can buy string at any good hardware store you know."

"This isn't string but a portable clothes line! What better thing could a man find than a portable clothes line? Look, let me show you how it works. It's not string but elastic and notice there are two strands wound around each other. All you have to do is hook the ends over a tree and tighten it. Then each bit of clothing is held on by opening up the two strands and pushing a bit of the clothing through. Is this not the find of the trip or not? Amazing eh?"

I was amazed; amazed that anyone could be so won over by a clothes line.

Brian had arranged to meet Trish at a Wahgunyah hotel, the Empire, and he assured me it was *the* place to celebrate his birthday with his good lady, and me of course, so we showered and dressed up in our finest.

The closest pub to the camping ground was actually in Corowa, near the famous Corowa Court House, where in 1901 a bit of a chin-wag was held, leading to the creation of the Federation of Australia. Up to 1901 there were six separate colonies, which apparently caused much confusion to the simple minded farming folk along each side of the Murray (the river being the border between NSW and Victoria). At a meeting in Corowa in 1893 - a conference where women were allowed to attend, but not to speak - a Dr John Quick successfully moved that each of the six colonies should introduce laws to provide for the election of representatives to a federal convention where they should consider and adopt a bill for a federal Constitution.

Apparently Quick added:

The best guarantee of popular interest, is that the people should be asked to choose for themselves who should frame the constitution.

A cry from the back of the hall was heard:

Like most great inventions that is simplicity itself!

A late working tradesman

Brian and I were simply after a thick slab of steak and to partake of the world's best ever invention - ice cold beer - but we gave the pub near the court house a miss and crossed the Murray into Victoria to have a meal at the not-so-famous Empire Hotel. Trish's sense of humour would have been sorely tested if she waited at the Empire for three hours while we wined and dined up near the court house.

Wahgunyah itself used to be famous, even more so than Corowa - at its peak it had seven hotels and was the busiest Murray port up this way - but today the Empire Hotel stands alone in Wahgunyah. It is an old style country pub with a dreary dingy bar at the front with two patrons who both gave

97

us a "G'day" as we walked through. Brian was keen to sit out the back where there was a tiny room set up for meals, with a few linoleum topped tables and wobbly chairs. There was no one else in this room, except a tradesman fixing a side door.

He greeted us as we walked in. Another "G'day." They are not big talkers in this neck of the woods, apparently.

I gave him back a smart aleck response: "Day."

"Could be a school teacher doing a bit on the side," said Brian quietly. "Can't be a real tradesman working at seven."

The guy had an electric sander, grinding down one side of the door. In this tiny room about three by three metres, conversation was difficult, even for Brian.

"Must be nearly finished," I yelled across to Brian.

"I bloody well hope so," he yelled back at me.

We knocked down a few beers waiting for Trish, accompanied the whole time by the hullabaloo from the sander.

"About time this bloody prick stopped and went home," Brian hollered back at me, just as the sanding stopped.

There was silence. I sipped my beer, studying the suddenly interesting pattern of the faded linoleum on the table top, waiting for this guy to start sanding down Brian's skull, but no, he was a pleasant country yokel.

He simply packed up his tools, mumbled "Day" and left us in peace.

Trish eventually joined us, making a grand total of three patrons at the Empire Hotel eatery that night.

While on the subject of food, Mitchell in 1836 compared the Australian aborigines with New Zealander Maoris in their liking for human flesh. He wrote in his journals that even though Australia was a land with little to offer the Australian savage was '*not a cannibal*' while the New Zealander, who had a far more productive country, '*notoriously feasts on human flesh*'.

Sturt however did hear of cannibalism amongst Australian aborigines. A stockman pointed to two men and said:

"That fellow, sir," said he, "who is sitting down, killed his infant child last night by knocking its head against a stone, after which he threw it on the fire and then devoured it."

Sturt tells us he was '*quite horror struck, and could scarcely believe such a story*' He questioned the men and one told him '*that the child was sick and would never have grown up.*'

Sturt was convinced by the story: '*as if I had seen the savage commit the act.*'

The Biggest Gum Tree

The next morning I looked through all our map books for this supposed world's largest red gum tree that Brian had mentioned. I saw many 'tree' notes in the book: 'Log landing', 'One Tree Bend', 'Tall Trees' and 'Big Tree Bend', then I read:

'Big Red Gum sixty metres. (986). This tree is reputed to be the biggest red gum in NSW and probably the world'.

Well, bugger me, it was true, the biggest red gum. It was near the Mallee Cliffs miles away up near Mildura, at the 986 blue distance marker, 1094 kilometres away to be exact. I could be dead before we were even close – the tree itself could be dead before we made it there - but I did make a mental note to take a photo of Brian at that 'Big Tree'.

99

After Corowa there was a passable current so we travelled well, averaging five kilometres an hour, stopping early at around four o'clock when we saw a camping site with all the creature comforts - trees for shade, a gently sloping grassy bank, a sandy bed by the water and of course the proverbial fishing hole nearby. According to the map we were in the Collendina State Forest, or I hoped so because we had camped on the New South Wales side and we did not want to be mistaken for a pair of bush hogs and be gunned down by a gun-toting red-neck farmer for sleeping in one of his cow paddocks. (Our map book reminded us, on every page that all private property bordering the Murray in New South Wales was privately owned a least to the water's edge, but Victoria has a 3chain (60m) crown reserve along the Murray.)

Now here is a snippet of legal advice: the actual state border between Victoria and New South Wales is not the centre of the river, but at the Victorian, the southern edge. By law - the Commonwealth *Separation Act 1850* defines Victoria as the land south of the Murray. As recently as 1980 the High Court of Australia had a look where the true boundary was, in an appeal case of *Ward v The Queen*. A trigger happy guy called Eddie Ward had been convicted in the Victorian Supreme Court of murdering a Mr. A. J. Reed. Eddie had fired from the Victorian side of the steep bank of the river down at Reed fishing by the river's edge, some thirty feet below. My guess is that Reed was fishing in Eddie's favourite fishing hole or he was too close to Eddie's shrimp nets. Eddie appealed the decision on the grounds that he was not in Victoria at the time he shot the guy. The High Court judges saw that the northern boundary of the State of Victoria was the top of the southern bank of the Murray River, so Eddie got off scott-free.

The Collendina State Forest, in NSW was as good a place as any for the day to end its run, a charming port of call so to speak. I read, dozed and even spotted the odd fish leaping up to tease my fishing partner. When a fish jumped I would call out whether he saw it or not, and whether it was big enough for us to eat for dinner.

Then a flock of cockatoos started circling around us, saying hello to each other and to us: 'Nice sunset, nice sunset, nice sunset.'

"I almost miss the guy with the sander," I said.

But soon darkness enveloped us, and the bush, so the cockatoos went off to bed. We sat by the fire looking up at the jet-black sky pin-pointed with umpteen stars and like little boys we became excited when a satellite whisked across or a falling star dropped down. The next morning I asked Brian if he slept well but he had not, saying it was too quiet once the cockatoos stopped.

This was not unlike Richard Burton when he was heading off to Mecca many moons ago. (He was in disguise, dressed up as an Arab because infidels get their throat slit if they are found even window shopping in Mecca). After a trek through the desert, they had '*arrived at their destination and camped with 50,000 other pilgrims on the slopes of Mount Arafat.*'

But at night Burton found that '*sleep was impossible*' because nearby '*an old man recited prayers throughout the night*', plus:

there were loud shouts of laughter from some Egyptian hemp-drinkers; and the sounds of wild Arab music accompanied by clapping hands could be heard all night long.

To Brian and I this would have sounded worse than a flock of cockatoos.

Geography lesson

We managed only 30 kilometres for the next day, passing the 2034 marker before we camped for the night. Then we headed off for Yarrawonga, with very little current to help us, since we were approaching the start of Lake Mulwala. We saw a river coming in from the south - the Ovens River, which gives the Murray some assistance, as do a few other streams. The main ones from the south are the Mitta-Mitta River which joined the Murray back before Albury (in the middle of Lake Hume), then after the Ovens River here at Yarrawonga we would be meeting the Goulburn River and the Campaspe Rivers which both come in near Echuca and then the Loddon River joins the

Murray near Swan Hill. These rivers come in from the south. From the north two large rivers join the Murray. First of all the Murrumbidgee adds its weight of water (after Swan Hill) and then the Darling River joins in. The Darling starts as a mere trickle way up north in Queensland; a few trickles in fact, the Warrego River, the Condamine River, and the Maranoa River to name a few. They all seem to merge then pass through the outback town of Bourke and slowly meander southwards through central NSW, before fanning out a little into Lake Menindee and a cluster of other lakes and pushing on down to where it finally flows into the Murray River at Wentworth in South Australia. Got that? If so, I should have been a geography teacher, like my paddling partner.

The original aboriginal inhabitants in this area, the Pangerang Tribe, named the area south of the river as Yarra - wonga, 'Yarra' means 'water running over rocks', and 'wonga' was named after the 'wonga pigeon' which apparently were as common there as cockatoos were around Howlong. Over the river, the area was called Mulwala, which means a big lagoon or big back water. Back in the 1840s there were believed to be over 12,000 members of the Pangerang tribe in the Yarrawonga-Mulwala region but within fifty years of the white man first swimming in the 'big lagoon', the Pangerang Tribe was gone from the region, forever.

Brian attempts to sell serenity

Brian and I gave the Ovens River nothing more than a quick glance before continuing on and soon enough the Murray had become Lake Mulwala where Brian and I followed the edge of the lake closely. To our right all we could see was a forest of dead gum trees in the lake, showing well-defined marks of water in dark stained rings on their bark-free trunks. To our left houses started to pop up and I wanted to find my friend Colin's house - all we had to do was find a pontoon boat. Most of the houses had a boat moored outside and we slowly floated by looking for something that vaguely resembled a pontoon, not that we knew what a pontoon looked like.

Finally we saw a boat perched on what could be a raft and Colin was as friendly, warm and hospitable as he ever had been, although he looked a little softer around the belly since I last saw him as a teenager. He offered us a beer, home-made, and a whisky, home-made. He then asked us:

"Why are you guys paddling down the river? That seems like a lot of hard work to me."

Brian tried to educate Colin on the esoteric values of kayaking down a river.

"Well Colin," he started, "it is worth it to see the beauty of the river from a kayak. It was a fast stream up in the Snowy Mountains but after Albury it had become a strong river bending and twisting its way along, with magnificent old red gums and sandy banks. We believe that down past Renmark, which is about a thousand kilometres from here, the cliffs and river banks are spectacular. Then there is the wild life, all the birds, the occasional kangaroo and the fish but most of all I love the serenity of the river. It is so peaceful."

He continued. "We don't see many people, we don't hear many people and as we are nowhere near any roads we don't hear any car or truck engines. The occasional boat we see is usually snuggled up next to a dead tree with a couple of close to dead codgers in it, fishing away for hours without a word to each other. All we can hear most of the time is the sound of our paddles hitting the water."

Colin digested all this and his first comment was: "Why don't you attach a whipper-snipper to each of your boats? You would fly along."

Chapter 9: 'measuring our distance'

[The river slows, and widens after Yarrawonga. We meet a brace of Germans, before reaching Tocumwal, where Brian kisses a very large fish.]

Distance travelled

The next morning we took one car further west along the Murray Valley Highway to his brother's place in Tocumwal, then it was back to Yarrawonga to restart paddling. I entertained Brian by singing him that well known World War 1 ditty:

I'm going back again to Yarrawonga
In Yarrawonga I'll linger longer
I'm going back again to Yarrawonga
Where the skies are always blue...

Below the weir the Murray had changed yet again, wider, and moving more slowly than before as it snaked its way around bends. Just outside the outskirts of Yarrawonga we passed a few campers, a handful of picnickers and a number of mighty sand banks with inviting grassy areas under grand old gum trees. The book told us we were in the Boomanoomana State Forest and soon to pass by Tungawonga and Cobrawonga Beach – captivating names.

The first blue distance marker sign we saw was the 1986 marker, which from the map book I saw that Tocumwal was at the 1880 marker so we (only) had 106 kilometres to go, for this leg, Tocumwal - three days of paddling. Now, this is as good a place as any to express my sincere thanks the 'Department of Blue Marker Signs' within the appropriate Government Department – they kept me sane, knowing where we were on the river and what distance we had travelled in a day.

Back in 1824 Hume and Hovell measured distance travelled using a sort of wheelbarrow. Hovell wrote on his first day out of Sydney:

At 1 p.m. left Mr. Hume's house in company with his cart; at 4 o'clock crossed the Cowpasture River, and commenced measuring our distance by perambulator.

This perambulator (wheelbarrow to you or I) they pushed along, and counted the number of times the wheel went round, and using the radius of the wheel, distance could then be determined by calculating the circumference ... all that stuff from school arithmetic. I have a hunch that neither Hume nor Hovell personally spent their time counting the number of times the wheel went around - they must have had some sort of odometer gear system and as one gear advanced to the next gear they knew a certain number of revolutions had gone by – plus a convict in tow with a notebook jotting down each click of the gear.

In 1836 Thomas Mitchell wasn't into perambulators. He had a different, and unusual, way of counting how far he had travelled: by counting the stroke of his horse's hoof. When he reached 100, he would put his hand into his pocket and remove a counter - a bean or a pea - and put it into his other pocket. He claimed that 950 paces of his horse made up a mile and after this he would take a new compass reading and start counting again. I can imagine Mitchell getting a little hot under the collar if one of his buddies hollered out "Hey Mitch, is it the 23rd or the 24th today?" causing Mitchell to lose count: "was I at 223 paces or 424 paces?" Possibly no one dared speak to Mitchell as he rode along.

Of course he and his men knew where they were, or roughly anyway, by checking '*latitudes determined nightly from observations of several stars.*' Mitchell also '*availed myself of trigonometrical measurements also with a good theodolite wherever this was possible.*'

Sturt, in his whaleboat, found it a little trickier to know how far he had travelled in a day but he managed, telling us that he used a compass and that he was a stickler for making sure he noted every turn in the river. Sturt was a busy man; he had to be as he was given the explicit instructions (by 'His Excellency Lieutenant General Ralph Darling, Commanding His Majesty's Forces, Captain-General and Governor-in-Chief of the Territory of New South Wales'):

You are to keep a detailed account of your proceedings ... describing the general face of all the countryside ... the nature of the climate, as to heat, cold, moisture, winds, rains, &c, .. the rivers, with their several branches, their direction, velocity, breadth, and depth, are carefully to be noted.

(Brian and I had it easy – we had blue signs on a gum tree two kilometres apart and we had no bugger telling us to describe *'the general face of all the countryside'*, only our wives telling us to keep away from red belly black snakes and well clear of any Swedish backpackers.)

Germans

Eventually we found ourselves alone on the river, except for a rust-brown wallaby that had come down to dabble his toes in the water, and by seven o'clock we found a hot spot to stop; and hot was the word, a scorcher of an evening, too hot even for Brian to fish, so we spent some time just lying in the river to cool down.

It may have been the heat or it may have been the locality but where we had stopped it was sand fly heaven and the little buggers were everywhere. We were not impressed. We had stopped too close to a cluster of reeds and as we both lay in the water, with our heads above water level, wearing only our hats and sunglasses, swarms of biting midges decided to feast on us.

107

Like a hippo I stayed in the river with the water up to the bottom of my nose and watched Brian putting up his tent. To ward off the sand flies he was dressed in long pants, long sleeved shirt, socks and shoes, hat, mosquito net and a liberal lathering of insect repellent. Eventually I had to join him, donning most of my clothing and pitching my tent, then wiping the dust off the dinner plates and whipping up what can only be described as an exceedingly tasty meal; Deb instant mashed potatoes and beef stew from a can, washed down with a few glasses of disgustingly warm red wine.

Near the end of the meal the Germans arrived, well the Luftwaffe did anyway. It started out as a dull roar in the distance like 100 large bombers travelling up the river flying at ten metres off the water; then the wingmen saw us and reported to their squadron lead: "White male flesh to the left Captain." "Attack!" was the Captains immediate reply. "Go in close, and when you think you are too close, go in closer". It was a squadron of mosquitoes, as large as bats and carrying barbed spears that could penetrate multiple layers of clothing. I lasted only five minutes before I retired to my tent, where a battalion or two of them circled around and around looking for an opening.

Brian lasted longer, at least another minute, before he had to retire to his tent. I could just hear him cursing and cussing away at one mosquito that had sneaked in with him.

"I have some spray here if you want to pop across and get it," I yelled out.

As usual our tents were over 50 metres apart so he decided to fight the Red Baron without outside assistance. Persistent whacking of a shoe on the ground was the last sound I heard before I dozed off. This was interspersed with a few comments that should not have made me smile, but did: "I will get you; you little prick, even if I have to stay up all night."

Of course we were hardly up against it, certainly when compared to Burton (and his companion Speke) as they battled their way across Central Africa in search of the source of the Nile. At one time near Lake Tanganyika they were both incapacitated. Speke had severe eye inflammation, and was *'sitting blind and in great pain on his donkey. Burton, his legs almost useless, had to be carried in a hammock.'*

Quiz Time

On the river it was warm and windless - with a current of two or three kilometres an hour – it was a day what the doctor would have ordered. We would drift down a short straight stretch of river then sweep around an attractive bend into either another straight stretch of the river, or immediately into another alluring bend. Each corner bend had a dollop of beach sand or small pebbles with massive white-trunked gum trees providing shade. We swam at our hourly rest stops and struggled to keep pushing on.

Tocumwal was now only sixty or so kilometres away and I felt this would be easily manageable, on the brink of being too easy and I even thought we could go on further from there this year. The past 10 days had zipped by, in part because at times we had resorted to mindless, childish and ridiculous activities to help pass the time as we paddled along together, activities like 'quiz time'.

Brian *loved* quiz time. He would start it with something like:

"Okay cocko, quiz time. AFL premiership winners. Who won the flag in 1990?" And off we would go, taking it in turns to ask then answer a question. Sport was a big quiz topic for us; possibly due to the fact that our combined general knowledge on any other matter was extremely limited

We camped on soft grass with Bondi-Beach sand down to the water and in the morning the sunlight peeped through the red gums shining some light through the grey trees to light up our camp site. The trees gave us some shade for a while but by late morning the sun was hitting every part of the river, however there were no complaints from Brian, or myself. Each day was just like the day before, another stunning section of the Murray River where the river curled around one bend then curled back around the next. It was serene and tranquil, with families of ducks like boats in the bath as our only company on the water.

Brian continued to visit the shore at times, searching for a platypus or a Murray cod in the roots of the trees exposed by the river bank or in snags from a fallen tree, which showed just above the water line. I would simply marvel at the red gums from the centre of the river, knowing that some were over 500 years old. That makes for an old, old tree.

Over, too soon

In the last day before getting to Tocumwal, just for fun, and to loosen up our limbs, we developed a lunchtime exercise routine, much like a Pilates class. We started with some knee bends while we had the first piece of unleavened bread with cheese, moving into squats with the second piece of bread with sardines or tuna and finishing with shoulder turns as we savoured a packet of warm peaches in syrup. Thankfully

10,000 camera carrying tourists didn't line the river banks - or we would have featured on Japanese late-night TV travel shows - 'Unusual customs of Australians'.

Brian and I turned yet another bend and there was a boat ramp, the Tocumwal boat ramp. This stage of the trip was over!

"How easy is this Murray River kayaking," I said to Brian. "I thought it would be more of a challenge."

I felt chipper as we pulled into the Tocumwal shore, so chipper that I was certain we should be able to finish the whole trip next year.

Now if you have never been to Tocumwal, the bright light is the Big Fish, a large statue of a Murray cod in the centre of town, which Brian had to give a big kiss before we departed our separated ways - Brian back 100 kilometres to Barnawatha and me 1200 kilometres to Coffs Harbour.

We had now paddled down 700 kilometres of the Murray; 'only' 1880 to go.

Phone call

That evening I called home. I was halfway, at Coonabarabran ('Coona'), in the back blocks of NSW, and booked in for the night at a budget Motel, one of many 2-3 star motels I could have chosen. Like a true male I did not check the price before booking in, or show my NRMA member card, or tell the motel people that my good wife holds a Platinum Card from the country women's wine buying group to get a 1% discount.

I thought Suzanne may query the room price ($65) so I told her it was late when I arrived and all other Motels were full. This was a sort of white lie - the other Motels looked full. I justified the price by explaining that the room did have a knockout view of the highway. 'Coona' like most country towns on the Newell Highway has the highway going right through the centre of town which made it remarkably easy to hear the truck air brakes at 3am.

I also explained to my sweet lady that the highway view was one of the better features of the room as the whole place was well past its use by date. A cockroach couple shared my pillow as I watched the TV. Many of the lights did not work which meant I had to wash myself and clean my teeth using the light from the TV reflected into the cupboard mirror and then into the bathroom. I did try the ancient air conditioner but it started shaking the flaky paint off the walls, so I turned it off and opened a window. Good God! I could all but touch the cars as they went by.

That was not all. Now remember this is the year 2007, the land of cable, and satellite TV reception, but not for the TV at this budget Motel in 'Coona'. TV offered five free to air channels but two had non-stop snowstorms showing, one had a sort of a picture with a flickering of movement and no audio and then there was the ABC with a discussion between a local parliamentarian whining on about the lack of water for the farmers in the outback of New South Wales, and that this was the Government's fault, not the farmers.

Suzanne then enquired if I had eaten.

"Yes, my dear. I have just wolfed down a mess of fish and chips bought from 'Coona's' finest café, washed down with three cups of sweet coffee which helped to dilute the litre of oil I was taking in with the fish and chips."

"You bought three cups of coffee?"

"No way. This place provides a kettle, three coffee satchels and three long life milk packets. This is not a two star Motel you know."

STAGE 3:

2008: It ain't no fun no more

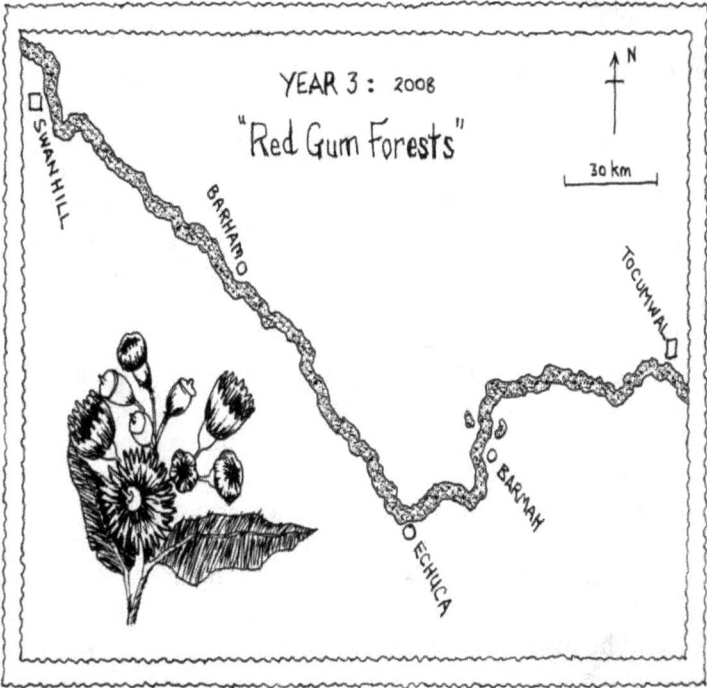

Chapter 10: 'never lighter at heart'

[Another twelve months go by before we are back on the river. Downstream from Tocumwal we see the original road base of Melbourne roads. Then we meet the cheery souls at the Barmah pub.]

Return to the 'Big Fish'

With three weeks available to us the following year, in February 2008, we aimed to cover 500 kilometres, from Tocumwal to Swan Hill, with the Murray now heading up into the north-western region of Victoria. There were only a few towns along the way, Barmah, Echuca and Barham, to break up the trip.

Brian and I were cracking up a little, physically I may add. I had been diagnosed with rheumatoid arthritis - my wrists, knees and ankles had become inflamed and swollen - so I was now carrying a few bottles of pills packed in with days of food supplies, plus our standard gear of tents, sleeping gear, cans of Guinness, bottles of red wine, fishing gear, camping chairs and a few litres of drinking water. And the quacks had found a small tumour in Brian's head, which was manageable, provided he took a special tablet once a week. Both our sweet wives suggested it may be a good time to call off the paddling plans but to quote Karel Čapek, a relatively unknown Czech writer from 100 years ago:

"Once you start... well, you don't have to start, but you have to finish!"

Sandy Beaches

Back on the river Brian and I felt free from care, away from people and the hustle and bustle of normal living. We were light at heart, shooting under the new Tocumwal Road Bridge and then under an old Tocumwal Railway Bridge, built a hundred years ago for the now closed railway line. It certainly was a delightful day as we dropped into our paddling groove. The straw-yellow sun beamed down on us, shut out now and again by rolling clouds overhead, and the whiff of a breeze helped to cool us down.

The Murray River around Tocumwal had a beach on every sweeping bend and massive river red gum trees. We camped for the night on 'Faraway Beach' near the 1862 kilometres to the end of the river marker sign. It would be hard to go past the sandy beaches near Tocumwal for a hunky-dory place to camp by the Murray. There are bucket loads of clean, soft sand leading up to a grassy bank with shade from clusters of gum trees. You could stand in the shallows and cast a line out into the river and catch a brace of fish, if you had the right know-how that is, or you could simply rest your weary old bones, which I did.

That evening I gave Brian a song book with the World's 20 best songs to sing - all in large type and each page in a waterproof jacket - and in return the kind man gave me a down pillow so I could stop being a martyr (his words), in using a shoe as a head rest.

We were much like Mitchell in 1836 on his first day on the road. He was riding on horseback with his men and he too was looking and feeling good. Descriptions of riding a horse in the Australian bush do not usually include the phrase 'bounding over hill and dale' but Mitchell used it as he clip-clopped along. He had doubts that he may not return to Sydney, but that did not deter the man from enjoying life:

We found the earth parched and bare but, as we bounded over hill and dale a fine cool breeze whispered through the open forest, and felt most refreshing after the hot winds of Sydney.

Yet, although the chance of misfortune flashed across my mind, I was never lighter at heart, or more joyous in spirit

Barmah-Millewa State Forest

The next day we had a south easterly wind behind us, with the river generally heading west most of the time. The superb sandy beaches up Tocumwal way had now been replaced by mud beaches, but in the late afternoon we easily dragged our kayaks up a gentle slope onto a flat spot and pitched our tents under some lofty gum-trees close to the edge of the river.

From our map book I could see nothing much to inspire me for the next day, apart from a bunch of bends: Thistle Bend where Thistle Creek comes in, Toni's Bend , Sixty Mile Bend and then we were in the Barmah State Park. A note told us that paddle steamers used to load red gum logs in these forests and transport them downstream to the sawmills at Echuca. Barges were loaded and set adrift to move downstream, with a chain dragging to keep them midstream, and they were eventually picked up by a steamer. (You may know that 60 Miles = 96 kilometres, hence the 'Sixty Mile Bend' was exactly 96 kilometres from Echuca.)

We paddled through the heart of the Barmah-Millewa State Forest which apparently makes up the largest river red gum forest in Victoria. It is often called a wetland as much of it is frequently flooded. The oldest river red gums are thought to be over 500 years old and we could see plenty that were over 30 metres high, some even reaching 45 metres, but nothing to match Brian's 'World's Largest Gum Tree' we were to meet up Mildura way

The river red gum tree (the *Eucalyptus camaldulensis* for those who like to be on the button) is not only found around these two forests but it lines the Murray most of the way. The trees are usually well over 20 metres high and a metre or more across the base, but the red gum would never be found at the front of the tree good-looks queue - it is a bedraggled looking specimen, with untidy patches of grey and black bark on a never-straight brown-black trunk, with branches that sprout out at any angle, devoid of any symmetry.

The Barmah-Millewa forest is one of the two largest river red gum forests in the world, the other being the Gunbower-Perricoota forest, also on the Murray after Echuca, so all going well we would be passing through there in a few days ready to spot the rare 'superb parrot' and the rarer 'regent parrot' in the hollows and spouts in the river red gum, not that I had a clue what these parrots looked like but Brian would know, for sure.

The Yorta Yorta aboriginal people, whose country includes this Barmah-Millewa forest, have their own story about how the Murray was created, it being a pretty significant river for Aboriginal people, as it has been for many a long day. Their story is that their God (Baiame) sent a giant snake to follow his wife as she travelled from the mountains to the sea and the path of the giant snake made curves, creating the river bed which was later filled with rain water to form Dhungala (the Murray River).

119

A wee bit more history for you: The Ngarrindjeri aboriginal people from the Lower Murray down Goolwa way have a different view on how the Murray was created. Their belief is that a few old timers of the Ngurunderi tribe chased a giant pondee (cod) down the river, trying to spear it. The pondee thrashed through what was then a small stream, widening it by the movement of its strong tail and thus creating the Murray River in what is now known as South Australia.

There was no end of these gnarled and curvy river red gum trees lining the river banks, and there were birds galore, a real shooters paradise if one was a shooter. Brian the bird watcher told me he had seen egrets, cormorants, spoonbills and ibis waterfowl and even an eagle or two – but still no mention of the 'superb parrot' and the even rarer 'regent parrot'.

The Barmah forest, you may like to know, provided the red gum bricks to pave the streets of Melbourne in the days before bitumen – the same rock hard bitumen which I had slept on for the last two nights because my air bed had become airless. I was hopeful we would get to Barmah soon so I could find a shop and buy a new self-inflatable bed.

The weather man kept smiling at us and it stayed fine and with only a breath of wind, so we headed off the next morning with the township of Barmah firmly in our sights. Brian scanned the sky for eagles, claiming to see two, and the water for pelicans (5), cormorants (4) and ducks (500). Ducks were there by the truckload, I could spot them.

Mitchell was very impressed with the method the aborigines used to snare ducks, *'a net suspended across the river between two lofty trees.'* The meshes in the net were *'about two inches wide, and the net hung down to within five feet of the surface of the stream.'*

Some of the aborigines would go up the river and others down, *'to scare the birds from other places and, when any flight comes into the net, it is suddenly lowered into the water.'*

The netting the aboriginals made almost knocked Mitchell's socks off.

Among the first specimens of art manufactured by the primitive inhabitants of these wilds none come so near our own as the net which, even in quality, as well as the mode of knotting, can scarcely be distinguished from those made in Europe.

(I too was impressed at our lunch break, not by any mode of knotting nets but by the fact that we were 10 kilometres from Barmah, making us 'only' 1772 kilometres to the end of the river.)

Barmah Pub

We were warmly welcomed by a gaggle of the local male workforce when we walked into the public bar of the Barmah Hotel. They seemed pleased to see some new faces in their pub, or maybe they were just a happy bunch, or they were just well into their fifth shout. They were dressed as many a tradesman is dressed, a well worn check shirt with well worn jeans, or in blue singlet and short shorts, standing in boots with brightly coloured thick socks. 'Straight out of Crocodile Dundee', I thought to myself.

Brian and I did stand out a little, me in my sunnies and thongs, with my old straw hat in my hand and Brian in his matching blue shirt and shorts, his face covered in white sun block.

"Hey guys, where you from?" asked one, the leader of the Barmah Hotel band of merry men.

Brian waved at me. "He's from Coffs Harbour and I'm from the Indigo Valley. We're paddling down the river. Started up in the Snowy Mountains near Khancoban and we're going down to Goolwa, to the mouth of the river in South Australia."

"River rats eh?" he christened us. Then he turned to his mates at the bar and shouted, "Hey guys, a couple of river rats here, going down the river to the end."

One of them looked at Brian's face covered in sun cream and asked him: "You a plasterer or are you into cocaine?" This smart remark created much hilarity with everyone at the bar, including me.

We enjoyed a beer, peering at stuffed Murray Cod mounted on the walls, news of local football teams and old black and white photos of red gum tree cutters and their log-laden wagons. Pictures of an old Barmah Australian Rules football team were nowhere to be seen but Barmah used to have a large indigenous population who could kick the ball a country mile. The earliest record of football being played at the nearby Aboriginal mission of Cummeragunja was in the 1880s. Back then they played a game they called 'Marn Grook' (Aboriginal word for football). Possum skin on the outer and the sinews of a kangaroo tail for the bladder made up the ball.

In 1899 the lads from Cummeragunja made up a team in the nearby Picola League and by all accounts were not too shabby, earning the title of "Cummera's invincibles". Other 'white-fella' clubs did not like having their butts whipped by these darker skinned boys so the other clubs voted that no player over 25 would be permitted to play for the Cummeragunja team - most of its champion players were old coots, well over 25 - so Cummera gave the Picola League the flick and resigned. Nothing like a bit of old racial prejudice is there?

Chapter 11: 'the blank hours'

[Tributaries add little to the water flow. We reach Echuca, once the king-pin town on the Murray. The current stops as we approach a lock, as does my enthusiasm.]

Meeting the once mighty Goulburn River

The next night we camped near the 1754 kilometres-to-the-end blue marker and I noticed that the Goulburn River joined us near the 1730 marker, only 24 kilometres downstream, a half a day paddling away.

I had to tell Brian, (mainly to take his mind off fish because he refused to believe that anyone had ever caught a Murray cod as big as one mounted in the Barmah pub):

"We've the mighty Goulburn River coming in to join us today Patrick, 24 klicks on, about four or five hours paddling. Hopefully there will be some water flow so it will be downhill sailing all the way from there. Echuca is only another 16 klicks after the junction so we could make it there tonight, that's if you want to rush and paddle hard so you can enjoy a shower."

We rushed and paddled, glancing at the Goulburn River when it joined us, both noticing it was no wide river, not by a long shot, more a withered stream barely trickling into the Murray. The name of this river started off as the Goulburn, (Major Goulburn was an ex-Colonial Secretary of the colonies), but the river name was later changed to the 'Hovell'. However the name 'Hovell' did not stick. The river then went through various name changes, such as 'Twisden' and the aborigine names 'Bayunga' or 'Bayungun' but all were given the flick by the locals ... and Goulburn it is today.

With the Goulburn River, Hume and Hovell feature again. Like the Murray River and the Ovens River they were the first pairs of blue eyes to see it. After they had crossed the Murray in

November 1824 they had continued south-west and on December 3rd Hovell wrote they met a broad expanse of water:

This river we named the Goulburn, in compliment to Major Goulburn. This river is as wide as the Hume where we first made it, say, eighty yards, but the current is not so strong.

Echuca and 'Maiden's Punt'

By late afternoon we reached the township of Echuca which is situated at the bottom of a deep bend in the river. Echuca is famous for its paddle boats and over the river in NSW is her sister town of Moama - famous for nought, as far as I could remember.

Moama was originally called 'Maiden's Punt' named after a James Maiden. I hope the Maiden family have a good scrapbook because James is a classic poor-boy-make-it-rich story. As a lad in England he stole a few silver spoons and candles and was shipped off to Australia. After four years his shackles were snapped off and he eventually ended up near where Moama is today. A smart cookie was our James as he realised not everyone could (or wanted to) swim across the Murray so he had a punt built. Apart from taking the ladies across the river so their knickers remained dry, it also took wool bales from NSW across the river - so they could go by wagon to Melbourne. He moved into punts in a big way, then cattle dealing and selling ale from his pub, the Junction Inn, and ended up a rich man. Good on him, I say.

In the mid 1800s Echuca and 'Maiden's Punt' were made pretty famous, by all the riverboat trade. Echuca was the largest inland port in Australia. Hume and Hovell, Sturt, and also Mitchell had set the scene for the white man to make good use of the Murray, and make good use of it he sure did. The aboriginal people shifted away from the river as the white interlopers with their sheep and cattle (possibly convicts on the run with some livestock they had filched) followed the tracks of Hume and Hovell down from Sydney.

125

These budding farmers slotted themselves onto prime land by the Murray. The first cattle station on the river was called Mungabareena, where Albury now stands, and the second Wodonga, on the other side of the river. In 1848 the Murray Downs Station of 600 square kilometres was taken up near present-day Swan Hill. In 1853 a section of the 'Wharparilla' run was leased, which is where Echuca sits today.

With farms and small towns popping up everywhere alongside the Murray a door opened up for any budding entrepreneur who could build a boat and develop some river trade. Bullocks struggled to carry wool bales when the tracks became boggy, and the pubs in towns liked to receive a new keg of ale once a week.

In 1851 Sir Henry Fox Young, the Governor of South Australia, saw value in using the Murray for inland trade. He offered a prize of £4000 for 'the first two iron steamers of not less than 40 horse power and not more than 2ft draught of water when loaded, that should successfully navigate the river from the mouth of the Murray to its junction with the Darling', to quote the Melbourne '*Argus*' newspaper report of the time.

The challenge was answered by a William Richard Randell. He realised that steam could do far more than boil a kettle to help produce a loaf of crusty bread (he worked on his dad's flour mill in the Adelaide Hills) so in 1852, with the help of his brothers, he began building a steamboat. The boys were pretty handy with a carpenter's saw bench and a pot of glue and the boat was launched on the Murray at Mannum in South Australia. They named the boat Mary Ann after their mother, as all sons would, (not name their boat Mary Ann but name it after their mother). William had achieved his ambition to be the first man to put a steamboat on the river but back in 1853 the Guinness Book of Records was 100 years away from its first publication so he missed out on his five minutes of fame.

Also hearing of the £4000 prize, and not to be outdone by the son of a mere baker, a Captain Francis Cadell commissioned the construction of a much larger steam ship, plus a barge which could carry tons of cargo. Ignoring his dear mother, Cadell named his vessel the Lady Augusta after the wife of the South Australian Governor, hence becoming the first toady in Murray River history. The departure of the Lady Augusta from Goolwa with the barge, the Eureka, was a big deal for the folks of 1853. Under an impressive by-line: 'Navigation of the Murray', the *South Australian Register* newspaper of Friday 26 August 1853 noted that at least 300 people had assembled to see the boats depart, including 'rural beauties and their stalwart companions'. Ah, nothing like a bunch of rural beauties to set a journalist's blood flowing in 1853, or the blood of a kayaker in 2008. The flag at the front of the Eureka bore a red cross, with four horizontal bars of blue, 'the cross being charged with five stars', as emblems of the different Australian colonies, while in the upper corner, in a token of British connection, was the Union Jack. It was named the Murray River flag.

Randell and Cadell raced upstream in their steamers from the mouth of the Murray at Goolwa, no doubt sledging each other as they chugged along. When they both reached Swan Hill, Cadell had enough and went back downstream but Randell took his boat on up to Echuca/Moama.

These pioneering voyages were the start of steam navigation for the Murray. For farmers there were two great benefits – one, their wool could be carried quickly from the river ports downstream to South Australia, without becoming grotty or being damaged on the way. But far more importantly, barrels of ale could be dropped off at the local drinking hole more frequently, which puts a big smile on the face of any farmer, (not bigger than when they receive yet another farming subsidy from the government, but big enough).

So from the time of Randell and Cadell the Murray River became a major inland highway. Paddle steamers and their

127

barges churned their way up and down the river carrying produce, dodging other boats carrying the week's mail and milk churns. The river was dotted with passenger liners, small fishing boats, ferries and even missionary boats such as the 'Etona' and 'Glad Tidings' which carried a man of the cloth, as in a priest or rabbi, who doled out religious services to lonely old souls along the river.

Within 20 years of the paddle-steamer race of the century, hundreds of river boats were bobbing along the river and other river towns such as Murray Bridge, Waikerie, Morgan, Wentworth, Barmah and Koondrook sprang up as ports for the rolling on of wool bales and the rolling off of beer kegs. Not that trade was limited to just wool and beer I may add; in truth everything from cooking pots, flour, tobacco, beer, galvanised iron, dried fruit, pipes, pickles, kerosene, candles, boots, books, saddlery, perfume, clothing and sewing materials was transported, possibly even noodles.

Times were good for the river boys of the 1880s but these good times did not last for long because a few smart people decided that freight could also be shipped around the place, and for less cost, by rail. In 1864, a train from Melbourne rattled into Echuca so farmers along the river in New South Wales then only had to ship their wool bales to the Echuca Wharf and within a few hours they were in Melbourne, ready for export. Not to be outdone by the Victorians in Melbourne, the South Australian government set up a new river port at Morgan with a rail line to Adelaide and soon a line from Melbourne to Wodonga was opened. Paddle-steamers started to lose business and the boom times for the Murray as a trade route had all but faded by the 1890s.

The townships of Echuca and Moama did not appear so faded to Brian and I as we drifted in, although a line of lifeless and listless paddle boats on the Echuca side all looked a little sad and unused, sleeping in the water five metres or more below the top of the river bank. The next morning we weighed anchor, or more accurately pushed ourselves off the bank, and headed off, passing by even wearier looking paddle boats taking a snooze from their recent labours. Just like old Grandma in a nursing home, the best days of these boats had long, long gone.

The next town on the river was Barham, 180 kilometres on. Barham that is, not to be confused, with Barmah which we have already been through. Barmah comes from the word Paama, an Aboriginal name for a meeting place for ceremonies, which the Barmah pub still is of sorts: as a meeting place for wise-cracking tradesmen. Barham has no indigenous ties but one of the first white grazers named his place Barham station after his wife's maiden name. What a good husband that man was. It was obviously not a trend many male farmers have followed, as our map book did not show a Val's Valley or a Harriet's Hill. If I had been around in the 1800's I would have named a lagoon 'Suzanne's Swamp'.

At our first rest spot for the day I noticed we were at the junction where the Campaspe River joined the Murray. It was but a trickle of a creek. What was it like years ago? It was much the same as in 2008, sorry to say. In the mid 1800s a Charles Rooking Carter in his book 'Victoria, the British "El Dorado"' or 'Melbourne in 1869' wrote that he went for a stroll one morning to examine the countryside near Echuca, describing it:

all flat land, and forms part of a great plain through which runs a never-dry river — the Murray.

Charles walked downstream to the Campaspe:

... a monster ditch, 30 feet deep, 100 feet wide at the top and 20 feet wide at the bottom... in some places contained no water, while in other parts here and there were detached pools of stagnant water.

129

More paddling

For me the joy of paddling diminished after Echuca. The river became wide in places - well over 150 metres - and with what seemed like very little current, I was dragging my feet, (or paddle), just dawdling along. If I stopped pulling I could see myself slowly drifting downstream, but if I didn't paddle it would take us weeks to get to Barham, not five or six days, as it should.

Brian did not seem to notice the lack of current, or the wide river, or the heat, or the flies, or any head-winds. He zipped along in front of me, commenting now and again on tree shapes or whacking away at a carp. After lunch I became a tired kayaker, yawning away and almost nodding off at times which caused the kayak to suddenly tilt over to one side. I drifted and floated along, sloshing along like a sloth and feeling quite lethargic. My backside was numb so I lapsed into a coma where I did not wish to talk to anyone.

"How are you going over there old son?" he would ask me. "Did you notice those cormorant's back there?"

I ignored him, but he persevered, as he did have a few kind bones in his body and he was a wee bit concerned about my well-being.

"Did you notice Murray short-necked turtles back there?"

I ignored him again.

"Did you hear the little plop when we scared them into the water?"

I saw nothing. There could have been a mermaid on a log and I would not have looked twice at her. Well possibly twice. Brian picked up the slight mood of depression in my voice; I think he could feel vibes that things were not too rosy with me so he jumped into quiz time mode. A quiz was the last thing I wanted to do. What I wanted was a helicopter to come down, pick me up and take me home.

He was not deterred. "Let's sing a song together from the song books."

So we placed the books between our knees and opened them at page one. 'I Got You Babe', by Sony & Cher, a great little ditty to start with, which we both knew well. Away we went, at the top of our voices, startling the hell out of all the wildlife for a 2 mile radius:

> *They say we're young and we don't know*
> *We won't find out until we're grown*
> *Well I don't know if all that's true*
> *'Cause you got me, and baby I got you*
> *Babe*
> *I got you babe*
> *I got you babe.*

Then we stopped. It was too hard to sing without some sort of accompanist. The 80 piece Australia Symphony Orchestra would have done us justice.

So we meandered on, and after lunch on one day we met 'Emmylou', who you will be disappointed to hear was not a Swedish backpacker, so the next few pages will not be filled with sex, drugs and rock and roll: 'Emmylou', in fact, was a big old paddle-steamer chugging its way up the river. The captain gave us a toot and we gave his passengers a paddle wave, then it was gone and we were back alone with the river.

And more paddling

Now paddling is an interesting activity, in one way. We did it for hour after hour, between eight and ten hours a day, for days on end, so you might think that it would be a perfect environment to ponder on the ills of the world; to solve world poverty, or resolve some long standing theory of Physics, or come up with something to match Shelly's poetry. But no, except for times when we discussed the sexual habits of the platypus or the variation in curvature of a young breast, my mind was blank.

All I could think was 'make this stroke smooth', because if the oar did not go in smoothly the kayaked rocked a little, and I needed a couple of strokes to restore its smooth motion. After making that stroke smooth I then thought 'make this stroke smooth'; and on and on it went, stroke after stroke, minute after minute, hour after hour. Such is the life of a long distance kayaker. It may seem romantic and glamorous and you may well envy us, but trust me, you can find better things to do with your day than spending eight to ten hours in a kayak. To brighten myself up I tried quietly singing a sea-shanty or two to help pass the time. 'What shall we do with a drunken sailor?' etc...

I cast my mind back 12 months when I said to myself: "How easy is this kayaking of the Murray River?" I must have been out of my mind! Did I really think we would finish the whole trip this year? Swan Hill now seemed like a perfect place to call it quits.

The wind became stronger on another afternoon and waves were hitting the front of the kayak hard. Short-term focussing became the order of the day, with very careful paddling when the water was rough so I did not flip over. Fortunately paddling was broken by our rest stops, which my knees and wrists continued to demand every hour. We would walk along the river's edge or scramble up the steep bank to see what we could see but the countryside was now looking decidedly parched. In most places the gum trees were far more stunted than further back up the river, and always slightly crooked, with bumps or knolls on their trunks. The ground was dry, as dry as dust, with the odd clump of dull brown-green grass matching the colour of the tree leaves.

Stick it – stick it

Sandy beaches and gentle shore gradients had all long gone so we camped high up on the river bank, five metres above the water, dragging one kayak at a time up the muddy slope. The ground was as hard as a rock and I bent half my tent pegs trying to whack them in. Of course I should not have been complaining about how hard this all was - there is a book *The Worst Journey in the World,* by a guy called Cherry-Garrard. It is the best one written about Scott's efforts to reach the South Pole a hundred years ago, if you are looking for a good read. Garrard describes they are man-hauling sledges for twelve hours a day in the Antarctic cold, and then agonisingly shovelling snow onto their tent skirting to hold it down when they camped for the night. All Cherry-Garrard could say for his own encouragement was, "stick it - stick it - stick it."

That evening we were joined by a friendly magpie, which gave us someone else to talk to. What I should have brought along was a book of poetry. As Cherry-Garrard in *The Worst Journey* says:

a volume of poetry was useful, because it gave one something to learn by heart and repeat during the blank hours of the daily march, when the idle mind is all to apt to think of purely imaginary grievances.

In the morning Brian asked me if I had heard a houseboat going by last night, which I had not, I hadn't heard a thing. He stood there with his hands on his hips and shaking his head, unable to believe that I could complain non-stop about his occasional snoring when I hadn't heard the houseboat. Apparently it was about 20 metres away, lit up like a downtown Christmas tree, with its horn honking and loud speakers blaring out Neil Diamond music, which is normally enough to wake the dead.

The river did not improve, well certainly not for a paddler like me looking for a fast current flow. We journeyed on, and on, forever and ever amen, it seemed, passing the 1650 marker sign, the 1648 sign, and the 1646 sign too. By the day's end we had crossed another 40 kilometres off the jobs-to-do-list. That evening we sat around our little campfire together, as always, mesmerised by the flickering flames licking away at the billycan.

According to the map book we had camped at One Tree Bend, not that many people can relate to where that is, but it is close to the 1638 kilometres sign to the end-of-this-bloody-river. Also marked in the book was a 'Lock 26' coming up; at a weir, the Torrumbarry Weir, only eight kilometres away. There was a kiosk marked and the good book read: 'for passage through the lock contact the resident lockmaster'. The wonderful book even had the phone number of the resident lockmaster! Brian had a phone so when we were close I would give him the number to call.

Chapter 12: 'please and thank you'

[With assistance, we skip around our first lock. Bird sightings and snake thoughts fail to take my mind off the drudgery of paddling. We eat a real fish.]

Molasses

We set off the next morning and I found it hard to get moving. We were paddling in water that seemed like treacle, but Brian explained to me that it was the backup from the lock, where the water is slow moving, if at all. There was certainly not much current, and we had a headwind just to make it harder.

It took us a couple of hours to go the eight kilometres to reach the Torrumbarry Lock and Weir, which the map book showed was 1630 kilometres from the end of the river. Then I thought: the book says this is Lock 26 so did that mean we had 26 locks to go through? Did that mean we have 26 stretches of water like this where the current flow is zero? As the main navigator, in that I was carrying the map book, I thought I had better check this out when we stopped at the upcoming Torrumbarry Lock and Weir. I also thought that if there were 25 more locks on the river I would be taking a bus home, at the upcoming Torrumbarry Lock and Weir.

Personally I blame a couple of Canadians for this bloody molasses we were wading through. 130 or so years ago, in 1884 to be exact, the Victorian Government started to look at how irrigation - the taking out some of the river water and flogging it to farmers - could work to produce crops, better crops and even some new crops, particularly in the north-west part of Victoria, the Mallee country. About this time a Canadian George Chaffey, who had been living in the USA growing oranges and lemons, helped make it all happen. In 1896 he was wandering around Victoria and visited Mildura, described by a Melbourne newspaper of the time as a '*Sahara of hissing hot winds and red driving sand, a carrion-polluted wilderness*'. But George squinted through the driving sand and saw a neat little fruit and vegetable garden watered by a windmill-operated pump from the Murray, much along the same lines as his own successful fruit gardens using irrigation in California.

Before long George and his brothers built irrigation systems near Mildura where channels carried the water (by gravity) after major pumping stations had been built to raise the water from the river up to the channels. But when the banks crashed in 1893, as they do now and again, Mildura land values dropped and settlers walked off the land. The good times were over for George, so he went back to California. His brother 'W.B.' Chaffey however stayed on, working his butt off to bring his orchard into production, which he did, even establishing the 'Mildara' winery and developing marketing procedures for dried fruits.

Irrigation in Mildura continued and this was all fine and dandy for a while, no one complained about the water diversion, or no one listened to anyone living downstream complaining, because they were in South Australia, a separate colony, which no-one in Victoria gave a hoot about. But eventually those in South Australia started to raise their voices in anger – in the dry seasons there was not enough water depth in the Murray for safe navigation and to make matters worse a drought period from the late 1890s until 1902 put a damper on irrigation. And so the states (states not colonies, as of 1901) met to discuss how to make the Murray River 'drought proof'. Their solution (in 1915) was to build a series of weirs and locks to manage the flow of the river for navigation and irrigation. They decided that 26 locks were needed and two weirs, the Hume Weir at Albury and the Yarrawonga Weir.

Brian and I were now at the first of these locks, number 26, the Torrumbarry Lock and Weir. There were a couple of buildings by the lock so we beached our kayaks there, where I found a guy wearing a khaki outfit. He had to be a ranger of some sort, or someone who had never grown up and liked walking around in a Boy Scout uniform. We had forgotten to make the phone call to the lockmaster, but this guy *was* indeed a ranger and most helpful too, explaining first that we could not get ourselves through the lock as it was not opened for small craft. Okay I thought; this will be a welcome message to pass onto Brian. All we have to do is carry our kayaks around the lock, not much more than 500 metres.

But the ranger, Darren Champion by name, was also a champion by nature: he had a tractor with a trailer to ferry our kayaks around the weir. Darren explained that there was only one more lock before Mildura and a few in South Australia – not the 25 we had feared. This good news I *could* pass onto Brian, who had meanwhile been searching out the kiosk to buy an essential item, a packet of Weet-Bix. He needed Weet-Bix because he was sick of muesli in the mornings, saying it reminded him of chook food.

Darren and his tractor eventually arrived, he dropped us just below the lock and away we went, with some dandy current at first which made paddling much more of a joy. The first session after the lock just whizzed by, but then the water flow slowed, my paddling pulse rate slowed in sync and my enthusiasm ground to a complete halt.

At about four o'clock we came upon a picturesque camping spot near the 1600 blue distance marker, a place with sweet green grass and a number of small trees for shade – this was a 10 out of 10 camp site but for some reason we kept going. Predictably, this was the last sandy bank with grass and small trees that we saw. Now cold and tired, I dropped further and further behind Brian while he stroked along, whistling at the birds and zipping into the bank at times to check out possible camping spots.

Only kangaroos and us

It was after 6.30 by the time we had stopped and the sun had gone on to punch a few of its UV rays at people to the west, so in the gloom we unloaded our kayaks. We were in a dense bush forest, with large gum trees above us, baby gum tree saplings at ground level, and piles of dead timber everywhere. The bush had an eerie feeling, of being untouched by human hand, as though we were the first people to have ever been there. It was dead quiet and we felt absolutely alone. There was no sign that anyone else had traipsed by: there were no roads, no tracks, not even an old rusted farmer's fence. We were in no-man's land, the good old Australian bush, alone except for a couple of kangaroos who gave us a quick glance before bounding away.

The next morning Brian asked me if I heard kangaroos during the night, but again, like the night that a noisy houseboat went by, I had heard nothing. He then showed me tracks all around my tent and the camping area, pawed tracks, looking horribly like a mob of kangaroos had stomped around for a long time.

Neither of us could understand why a mob of kangaroos doing a corroboree, playing didgeridoos and singing a Rolf Harris song outside my tent had failed to waken me.

Birds

We were at a place called Halfway Bend. "Halfway to what?" I wondered, but I couldn't be bothered to work it out. We had just passed Kate Malone Bend and too, likewise I couldn't imagine why it was called Kate Malone Bend. I looked at the next 40 or so kilometres and neither a river nor a wee creek joined the Murray. I noticed a few lagoons marked when we passed through the Gunbower State Forest, and also a number of clay bars, which I guessed would be of no concern to us.

I was fast losing interest in the river, and any enthusiasm I may have had to reach the Murray mouth at Goolwa had gone, gone, gone. My days started to become more and more focussed on the distance markers. On this day we started near the 1546 sign, and by the end of the first hour we had passed the 1539, then past the 1534 in the second hour, the 1530 in the third, and so on. We managed four or five kilometres each hour which was progress, slow progress I may add, but progress all the same.

After lunch I would drop further behind Brian but good lad that he is, he would wait for me. We tried a nature competition to help pass the time giving ourselves one point for every bird and up to ten for each snake we spotted. This was fine; it gave me something to look for as we coasted along, to take my mind off the paddling. Within 10 minutes Brian had seen a blue kingfisher (one point), a speckled warbler (two). Personally I didn't know a duck from a speckled warbler.

Brian and the explorer Hovell would have got on well, because Hovell loved birds too. He wrote in his journal that the *'bronzewing pigeon'* was not as common as the black and white cockatoos and the parrots, and where there was water he saw *'curlew and snipe'*. I reckon that Hovell would have whipped Brian's butt in a bird watching competition - Brian never mentioned that he saw a curlew, let alone a snipe.

"Cockatoo," Brian cried out, pointing up in the sky. "Three points."

140

Snakes

I thought my best bet would be to look out for a snake and collect 10 points in one go. That would blow Brian out of the water, so I shifted over close to the bank and actively looked for some snakes. But did I see one? Nope. Not one. Did Brian ever see one? Nope. Not one. Where had they all gone? Except for one small snake we saw crossing the river up near Walwa on the Upper Murray, we have not seen one.

"Keep looking old son. It's the only chance you have because I'm now up to seven points. I have seen seven different birds."

We carried on two conversations, ignoring each other.

"Did I tell you Patrick that my sweet wife is concerned about me being bitten by a snake?"

"The last one I saw was a thornbill. Beautiful bird."

"She asked me what I would do if I was bitten. How would I get to a hospital? She was worried that you wouldn't have phone cover in some places so we wouldn't be able to call for help."

There were no birds around so he joined in my conversation. "Your wife worries about you too much. Let's get moving. I need to see an owl or a parrot."

We floated on but I kept thinking about snake bites. I had not thought about this too much so far, but the more I thought about it the more I started to worry. What would I actually do?

I asked Brian what he would do if I was bitten by a snake. I knew the latest snake bite treatment involved simply immobilising the limb and waiting for help, so I imagined myself lying by the river bank, leg in a splint, life slowly ebbing away as we waited for a boat to go by. Brian told me relaxation was the best remedy so he told me he would fish all day while reassuring me with comments like: "Just relax old son. Don't get agitated. Someone will be along soon to rescue us. Or rescue you should I say. Don't move around. Don't let anything worry you as this will only get the blood moving and stir the poison up, moving it closer and closer to your heart."

I then told him what I would do if he was bitten by a snake. Thinking about this gave me some perverse pleasure as I travelled along. I would strangle the snake first of course, or whack it with my paddle to show the hospital so they could inject him with the right anti-venom. I would strap up his leg with one of his many shirts, lay him in his kayak, with the dead but still wriggling snake as company, attach a rope to his kayak and tow him to safety. If I played my cards right I could have a

TV crew waiting for me as I rowed into town; even an interview with a sexy news reader.

We carried on this delightful fantasy for quite a while. It helped pass the time and gave us a chuckle now and again.

He told me that if I died he would simply wrap me in my sleeping bag and dump me with the first person I met. What a friend! How could I top that? So I made up a story that I would carry his body out, either in his kayak with me towing him, or by throwing his body across the front of mine, like an old wheat sack. To stop him stinking I would cut his heart out and wrap him in some branches from a gum tree, or with reeds. I had read that when the Scottish explorer David Livingstone died in the middle of Africa, a couple of his porters cut his heart out and buried it, then embalmed the body by rubbing salt into his skin and leaving it in the sun to dry out, then wrapping it up in bark and sealing it up with tar. They then carried him out on a pole, and went with the body all the way back to England.

My still very much alive partner (Brian) didn't seem to be listening to my story as he suddenly pointed up and yelled out, "Parrot!"

I tried to get his mind back onto snakes. "Did I tell you Suzanne and I went to a boating store and asked about boat rescue communication systems that would allow us to get in contact with anyone, from anywhere? They were talking hundreds if not thousands of dollars. Then the guy in the shop said: Why don't you just use your phone? Telstra has coverage just about everywhere in Australia and certainly along most of the Murray River."

On hearing this Brian quietly said, "That guy in the shop has more intelligence than you and your wife put together. I do have a phone, so if you happen to get bitten I will just phone for help."

Good point I thought, but I vowed to take Suzanne's mobile phone with me in the unlikely event I was back on this river again. We stopped that night with about 60 kilometres to go to Barham, at a place called Cemetery Bend which sounded to me like a bad omen so I told Brian to be on the lookout for snakes, and for both of us to whack the ground as we walked around. Vibration, we both said. Snakes have no ears, they go by vibration.

I started walking around dragging my feet on the ground and stomping as noisily as I could, but we soon forgot about snakes and carried on as normal, hitting the sack just after the sun slipped away, and sleeping as soundly as ever.

We had now reached that part of the river where Mitchell had been – he had been following the river upstream. Perched on the top of a hill only a few miles from where we were he saw a hill, which today is called Pyramid Hill:

A remarkable hill of granite appeared 5 1/3 miles from Mount Hope, bearing 30 degrees 10 minutes West of South. It is a triangular pyramid and, being quite isolated; it closely resembles the monuments of Egypt.

(So the next day Mitchell bade farewell to the Murray as he rode off west into the sunset, or, south to be precise, to the coast).

Here is a little more news on Mitchell, after he left the Murray. He headed off south west and reached another river, the Glenelg, and rowed south (in a boat carried along in one of his bullock carts, which all good horsemen carry in case they meet a river like the Glenelg). When the river reached the sea on the south coast he found the Henty brothers, not that he knew the Henty boys were there. Finding some white fellas surprised Mitchell - he didn't know that the Henty family, the first Europeans to settle in Victoria, had come across from Tasmania (or Van Diemen's Land as it was then known).

144

In his journal Mitchell wrote: '*I was much more astonished ... of the fresh tracks of cattle ... and the shoemarks of a white man.*'

He was '*struck with the resemblance to houses that some supposed grey rocks under the grassy cliffs presented*' before realising that these were in fact wooden houses.

He had stumbled across the farm of the Hentys:

... a man came towards us from the face of the cliffs. He informed me in answer to my questions that ... just round the point there was a considerable farming establishment belonging to Messrs. Henty, who were then at the house.

The Henty brothers had been settled on the southern coast two years before, raising sheep and cattle and catching whales. After a day or two of rest, and possibly sunbaking and surfing in the sea with the Henty boys, Mitchell headed back to Sydney. The Hentys had no doubt fed him on the best lamb shanks and beer-battered whale-fillets Thomas had ever eaten. Or at least, by his account, he was:

... accommodated with a small supply of flour by Messrs. Henty who, having been themselves on short allowance, were awaiting the arrival of a vessel then due two weeks.

They also supplied us with as many vegetables as the men could carry away on their horses.

Break-down

The next day Brian and I said farewell to Mitchell's departure point as we sloshed our way down the river in a westerly direction, with Barham in our sights. From now until the end of the Murray we would be travelling in Sturt or Mitchell country. In 1836 Mitchell's team followed the Murray closely from the Darling junction, back up to this point. And when Brian and I arrived at the Murrumbidgee, we would be

145

travelling downstream on the same water as Sturt and his men did, in 1830.

Our mid-morning paddling was interrupted by Brian's kayak suddenly going left and he yelled out: "My rudder is not working. Let's paddle over to the bank and look at it."

This was our first little breakdown. His rudder cable was broken, down inside the kayak near the foot pedal, but Brian was prepared for any eventuality and he had brought along wire and a pair of pliers, telling me in no uncertain terms, and more than once, that they were essential items to take on any trip, and for me to remember that. He thought you could do anything with wire, pliers and duct tape. I did wonder if he could fix a rudder cable, but he could, wrestling away down inside the front of the kayak. My job was to pass him the pliers, or bits of wire, which I did by saying:

"If that pleases you my good friend," or "I will without complaint," or "I will keep up my good grace with you all day."

Now, unsurprisingly, these waffly-words did not go too well with my good friend, wedged inside the kayak.

"What in the hell are you on about?" he would call back at me.

"Did I ever tell you about three guys in Antarctica? They are in a bad way, slogging along in minus fifty degree temperatures, in pitch black, in mid-winter trying to get some penguin eggs from a rookery hut. This guy Cherry-Garrad tells us that they:

did not forget the Please and the Thank You, which means much in such circumstances, and all the little links with decent civilization which we could still keep going. I swear there was still a grace about us.

146

"Only a Brit would write that sort of crap. Pass me the duct tape, if you please."

That afternoon we put in some hard yards, travelling north-west with a strong breeze blowing at us from the west. Brian loved it when the water was choppy and the wind was strong. Occasionally I would look across at him and the prick just seemed to be gliding along, zipping through the waves, not getting wet, seemingly not under any hardship at all. At the end of each bit of hard yakka he would wait for me. He always looked pleased with himself. "Great stretch of water there eh? I think that bit of the river was close to eight hundred metres wide and we were directly into the breeze."

It was a cool day so I started to shiver and shake whenever we pulled over for a stop. I hopped around, did some exercises, swung the arms and did knee bends all in a vain attempt to get warm before we started paddling again. Brian was quite impressed with my callisthenics but he could not work out why I was soaking wet when he was as dry as a bone. We put it down to the way I was paddling, or possibly my cheap plastic paddle was to blame, which Brian was now certain belonged with a toy canoe, not a river kayak.

Mitchell on his travels was chilled on many occasions, and in his journals he compares he and his men with the local aboriginals, calling the paragraph, 'Different Habits of the Savage and Civilised'. He describes how *'fire is the only means he possesses to warm his body when cold'* whereas Mitchell's men *'require both fire and clothing.'*

Mitchell was a good man with the pen, making many interesting notes on Australian life, in 1836. He once described watching an aborigine, unaware of his presence. Mitchell wrote that he was seeing *'the habits of a savage man at home'*, and he was fascinated:

His hands were ready to seize any living thing; his step, light and noiseless as that of a shadow, gave no intimation of his approach; and his walk suggested the idea of the prowling of a beast of prey.

Mitchell then called out, with *'a loud halloo'*, and the man then stood still, looking at Mitchell for about a minute, before he *'retired with that easy bounding step which may be termed a running walk.'*

A Fish (finally)

Brian and I were now in the New South Wales Koondrook State Forest, so tonight we could pick a spot to camp on either side of the river, which in reality gave us the choice of a steep, muddy bank to our left or a steep, muddy bank to our right. We chose the right hand side for no other reason than to be in NSW for a change.

Later on I noticed that Brian could not get any reception on his phone. "Watch out for snakes," I told myself. "Watch out for snakes," I told Brian too as he wandered off in the evening gloom, once again trying his fishing luck using shrimps caught in his shrimp net. I sat down and made a note of good things to bring on a kayaking trip. I never intended to go on another kayaking trip, but it was a way to pass the time.

First: a good collapsible bucket. There may be no greater gift known to a kayaker, other than finding a whipper-snipper, than a collapsible bucket. They hold over five litres but squash down to nearly nothing when empty. We had one each but Brian's, surprise, surprise, was better than mine. Mine was meant to be a 'Stand on its Own' bucket so that when you filled it with water it sat on the ground like a normal solid bucket. Ingenious I hear you say, and it was, almost. It stood for a while, but when you looked back two minutes later there was five litres of water on the ground around the collapsed bucket. I learnt not to trust the 'Stand on its Own' claim and hooked it over a tree branch.

I abandoned my note of good things to bring when I heard a plaintiff cry from Brian, something close to a blood curdling scream. My kayaking partner is in trouble I thought. A snake has got him was my guess. Don't panic. Immobilise the limb. Cut out his heart. Wait for help.

But joy of joys it was no plaintive cry for help, but the cat-call of a successful fisherman. There he was, with his head light shining on a fish that looked at least 30 centimetres long, his clackers sparkling in the light of his torch. Brian's teeth sparkling that is. The boy had a smile from ear to ear.

"Can fish!" he hollered. "Eat all your words of criticism McOrist as you cast your weary blood shot eyes over this beauty. It is a yellowbelly, big enough to eat and beautiful to eat. Breakfast tomorrow is on me."

Well, thank the Lord Jesus for that I thought, he has finally caught a fish. I did give him a short round of applause. Was he pleased? Apparently.

"Get the camera. This is a picture worth framing," he hollered.

149

We shared our one hooked-by-shrimp fish for breakfast and exceptionally tasty it was too, and certainly a welcome change. The next day was a lot warmer and the sun brought out some wildlife, not a lot, but some: a few river turtles tanning up their bodies as they sun-baked on a log, a couple of emus who had wandered down to the river for a dram or two of river water.

We hadn't seen a lot of wildlife, before then. Turtles plus emus made it a big day for seeing something because most days we saw little - the occasional wallaby and once in a while a big red kangaroo, but many days had gone by where we saw nothing, but bird-life. There may have been a crocodile in the mud, eyeing us as we floated by, or dingoes by the dozen slinking through the grass, but we were none the wiser.

Not surprisingly back in the early 1800s there was wee bit more wildlife around. When Mitchell passed through this part of the country in 1836 he mentioned seeing many kangaroos, emus and dingoes:

150

On the largest plain crossed by the party four emus appeared, and one of them was killed after a fine chase by the dogs.

Kangaroos were more numerous in this part of the country than in any other that we had traversed. I counted twenty-three in one flock which passed before me as I stood silently by a tree. Two of the men counted fifty-seven in another flock.

Sturt in 1830 was always on the lookout for emus, for food. He wrote on one day:

We were just about to land, to prepare our dinner, when two emus swam across the river ahead of us. This was an additional inducement for us to land, but we were unfortunately too slow, and the birds escaped us.

Chapter 13: 'this ain't no egg shop'

[A girl's left breast and country music brighten our day. Back on the river we see almost no one, and eventually we reach Swan Hill. Was it the end of paddling for me?]

Recovery at Barham

Brian and I hauled our kayaks up a grassy bank at the Barham camping ground, opposite the spot where the Gunbower Creek joined the Murray. We noticed that this creek did not add one drop of water to the Murray flow, but we soon forgot about water flows because we had the joys of civilisation waiting for us, as in a washing machine and a hot shower.

Like many a town on the Murray, Barham in NSW had a sister town over the river in Victoria, Koondrook in this case. Koondrook is a name I liked. It had a certain ring to it. Koondrook is an Aboriginal word for 'meeting of the waters', but I suggest it should be deleted from all aboriginal dictionaries. We had seen first-hand that there was no 'meeting of the waters' here – a nearly waterless Gunbower Creek met the Murray River at Barham.

At the Barham Hotel, we blended into the crowd because Brian's face was washed of its layers of white zinc cream. Not that the crowd was huge, a few regulars staring at the spirit bottles behind the barman, as regulars tend to do, and one other sitting down with his girlfriend, who had the most beautiful looking breasts we had seen for a week. Brian was smitten, and as he sat there in a glazed trance staring, I started to understand how he had managed to get his nose punched a couple of times in his life.

One of the regulars came up to him, and I sat there anticipating a left hook to Brian's head or a heckle like: "Stop staring at my sister's tits."

152

But no, it was only a friendly: "Hey guys, where are you from?"

Brian, slowly and reluctantly dragged his eyes off the girls left breast and - always prepared to strike up a conversation - replied, "We are paddling down the Murray. Started up in the Snowy's and are on the way down to Goolwa."

One crusty old coot shook our hands, and said:"Well done guys. Please to meet ya. Me name's Slim."

"Mine is Brian, and this is Wilson. That is his first name."

Another guy shook our hands and introduced himself:

"Hi, I'm Stuffy."

Brian could not help himself with a smart crack back: "Are you? Well I am just a normal person."

Fortunately Stuffy had had a few beers and this smart arse reply, which I thought was quite funny, went right over his head. Just to be safe, I stood up and dragged Brian out to go shopping before the supermarket closed and before Stuffy (or the barman, or the brother of the girl with the one in a thousand breasts) laid one on him.

Later that evening, in dire need of other human company of any sort, we joined 200 grey haired folk at the Barham and District Services Club where we were entertained with 1950's Country & Western songs, sung by none other than old Seekers singer Keith Podger. Such are the places ex-famous singers end up, like the Barham and District Services Club.

By the end of the evening we were chipper, the beers helped, the meal of fish and chips helped, the Country music even helped, but being surrounded by 200 grey haired old cronies made us feel younger, and this certainly helped most of all.

153

Map man

At ten the next morning we were still just as chipper. We coasted along in relative quiet, the only sounds being the slap-slap of our paddles into the water - the river was delightful to be on again. We slowly ambled along, clicking over the two kilometre blue distance markers. I would look at the map book at most rest stops but then forget what I had read half an hour ago so when I was back in the kayak, and I wanted to know what lay ahead, I had to stop paddling, get the map book in front of me, change my sunglasses for reading glasses, find where we were, look at what was around the next few bends, store that in my memory banks, change my glasses, and put the book away. By this time Brian was 200 metres ahead of me so he had to wait to allow me to catch up.

"How are you going old timer," Brian asked me as I caught up to him.

I held up the map book. "The good book tells me that there is an 'old boiler' coming up at around the next bend."

154

"Fascinating. You do realise that at this rate of travel we will be on the river for another month?"

Later that evening we sat around the fire, sipping a tea-cup of cask red, listening to the ABC country radio. We discussed why we were never extremely hungry at the end of each day. This day, like many others we had pulled on the paddles for over eight hours but we had eaten only a small breakfast of Weet-Bix with fruit, then a few chocolates, muesli bars and raisins, and lunched on two pieces of unleavened bread with cheese and sardines. By all rights we should have been ravenous by evening meal time. But we weren't. For most evening meals we ate our little tub of noodles, just one each, supplemented with a share of a small packet of dehydrated vegetables, but after that we were done.``

That night was full of excitement; well it was compared to most other nights in that I heard a pig squeal. I found out the next morning Brian had scared the life out of a wild pig when he went off for a bog, or the pig scared the living daylights out of Brian more likely.

People

Except when paddling near a town we had seen no one on the river, except for the occasional fisherman asleep or dead in a small boat, a couple of water skiers, and a few merry men (and women) on a paddle boat. We hadn't even seen a soul in a kayak or a canoe travelling along the river, which surprised us.

155

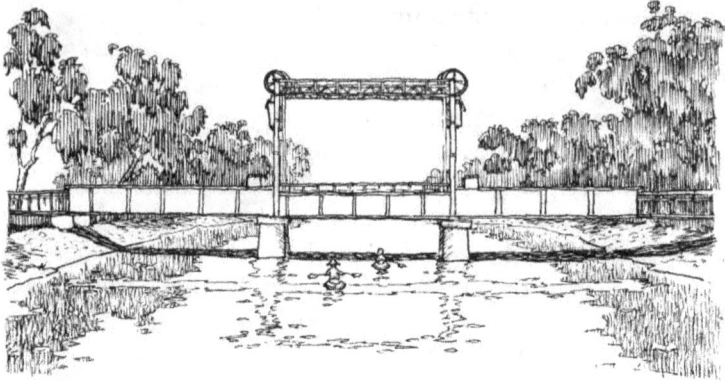

Later that day, we slid under the Murrabit bridge where a couple were fishing; well the guy had hold of a fishing rod and his female partner appeared to be just sitting in the boat with him, which must have made for an exciting few hours for her. So our presence brightened up her day, as brief as it was, as we only took 20-30 seconds to go past them. The lady in the boat asked me: "Where are you guys going to?"

I gave her my stock standard reply: "We are doing the Full Monty. We are going all the way."

And that was typical of the high quality communication with the occasional fisherman, or his good wife.

My first sensible question to a fisherman was usually: "Caught any fish?" They always said no. Fishermen never say yes when they are asked this question. Why? Because others may stop and fish in the same place – and this destroys the theory of fishermen being decent people. Just to annoy Brian I would often say: "My mate says he can fish but he has only caught one fish in six weeks."

Our sanity

The hours went by without much to interest us except the rare sight of a large goanna 40 metres up a gum tree fighting a

156

cockatoo for her eggs. We did not see one koala, much like the early Australian explorers who had similar trouble. The first recorded account of the koala was in 1798 when a servant to the governor of the colonies, Governor Hunter, wrote that they had heard of '*another animal which the aborigines call a cullawine*' which was thought to be a monkey. Four years later a Francis Barrallier in Sydney wrote about the first evidence of the koala, having seen two of its feet pickled in rum.

Without fail though it was carp that still interested Brian, now trying to spear them with the end of his paddle rather than wop them on the head with it. I told him he should make a real spear, by cutting a branch off a tree and tying one of his fifteen fishing knives to it. I thought that would make great carp killing implement.

Back in the 1800s the aborigines used their spears as canoe paddles. When they launched their bark canoes, which was the only frail means they possessed to cross rivers with their children. They would use their spears which were about ten feet in length, as a pole, bending them nearly double in the water. This was sort of like Brian, but he used his paddle as a spear, rather than using a spear as a paddle.

Another lone, ever inquisitive magpie watched us eat our evening meal – that night a can of braised meat, which was hopefully cow - which we both savoured as a luxury item, especially as we still had a cup of red wine to go with it. The red turned the braised beef into filet mignon.

We would then spend an hour or two staring at the stars, carrying on a highly intelligent conversation.

"I read about two guys who kayaked to New Zealand. Took them nine weeks."

"Crazy," said Brian. "How could anyone keep Guinness cold for that long?"

"What surprises me is how they managed not to kill each other, being cooped up in one kayak for that long."

"Couldn't someone tell them there is now an airline service to New Zealand?"

"Well, I hear there's a bus service from Swan Hill to Goolwa," I added.

We set off on our last morning with only 20 kilometres to Swan Hill, so Brian put on his best shirt and both of us were in high spirits. I hoped we would not be delayed, because we were down to one packet of dehydrated beans. We passed a stream coming in from the left as we neared Swan Hill, but neither of us was interested. In actual fact it was the Loddon River and we should have been interested because Mitchell camped there in June 1836. His camp site was near a hill *'between the two rivers.'* Half a mile away from their camp there were many swans and other wild fowl and Mitchell tells us that *'their noise disturbed us through the night.'*

Because of the noise of the swans he named the place *'Swan Hill, a point which may probably be found to mark the junction of two fine streams.'*

Swan Hill

So that is why Swan Hill is Swan Hill, and by early afternoon we were there, drifting up towards the boat ramp at the camping ground. Well, I may have been drifting but Brian raced there at full speed, like a kayaker out for a quick Sunday morning paddle. I let him go. As he approached the ramp he took off his kayaking hat with the flaps at the back and sides and combed his hair. An old guy fishing by the boat ramp would have been impressed by this neatly hair-combed, well-dressed looking kayaker.

Fifteen minutes later I joined him. We shook hands and congratulated each other, even asking a passer-by to take our photo. Brian was a happy man.

"Well, that was an easy 500 kilometres. We now have only 1400 to go. Almost halfway."

He told me he was surprised I had made it with a child's plastic paddle, and suggested I spend some of my millions to buy a proper one before next year. "Next year," I thought? No way.

Brian strolled over to the camping store kiosk to get his car keys and his car, while I rested under the shade of a big old tree. Possibly it was a coolabah tree, but I'd given up caring. I was happy to relax and recover; hoping Brian would take his time before he came back. I kept mumbling to myself, 'never again', 'never again', that should do us I thought - I had had enough. For me it was quits. We have made it all the way from the Snowy Mountains up to Swan Hill, which was not a bad

159

feat in my eyes. Over 1000 kilometres would impress all our friends, as not one of them was at all interested whether we made it to the end of the river or not.

Brian came back with the car and before I could say 'let's call it quits' he put his arm around my shoulders and began prattling on: we had made Swan Hill, we now had less than 1500 kilometres to go, next year we should try and finish it, repeating his desire for me to get a new paddle.

I said nothing. I feigned some enthusiasm to keep him happy hoping like hell this moment of madness would wear off when he got back home or that some guy in a pub would rip his arms off for staring at his girlfriend's breasts. That would make kayaking difficult, even for Brian.

We adjourned to a Swan Hill hotel for a couple of celebratory beers. Brian looked around at the half dozen yokels slouched at the bar.

"Don't these people realise who we are? Don't they realise they are in the presence of greatness? Don't they realise that they are in the presence of two heroes who have kayaked from the Snowy Mountains all the way to Swan Hill?"

No, they didn't, which reminds me of my mate Cherry-Garrard. He was the only one of the three guys who went off for penguin eggs that survived. The other two died with Scott coming back from the South Pole, but eventually Garrard got back to England and took the eggs to the Natural History Museum where the great response he got was: '*Who are you? What do you want? This ain't an egg shop.*'

Then Brian and I were off home, via the Barmah caravan park to pick up my car and trailer, and then a 1200 kilometres drive back to Coffs Harbour for me, via the back-blocks of central NSW. Suzanne asked me if we had a good trip and of course I lied and told her it was first-rate. I also told her I could hardly wait to finish it off next year, which was an even bigger lie.

160

STAGE 4:

2009. Compared to others, our life is rosy

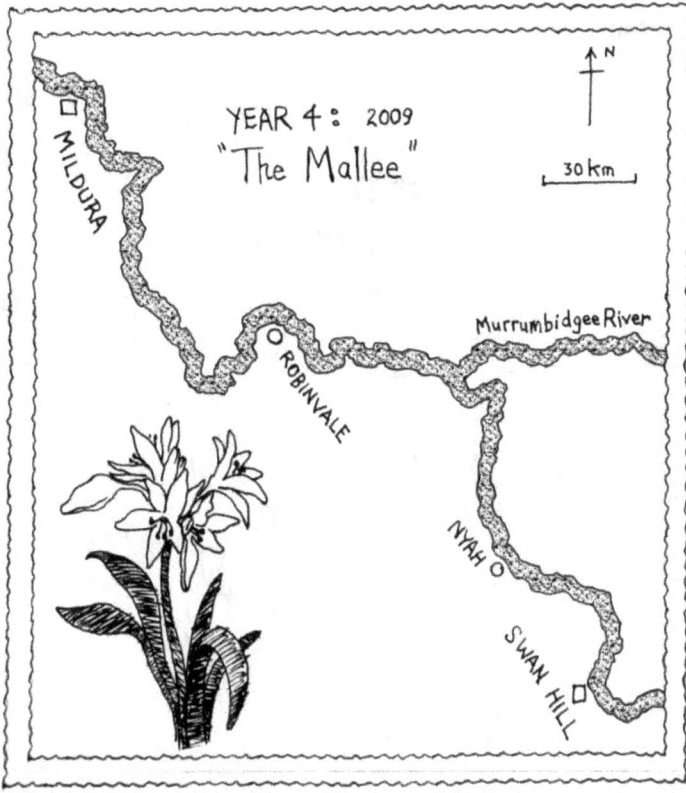

YEAR 4: 2009
"The Mallee"

N

30 km

MILDURA

Murrumbidgee River

ROBINVALE

NYAH

SWAN HILL

Chapter 14: 'intolerable weather'

[Brian and I, and a heat wave, meet at Swan Hill. We see many animals by the river. The township of Nyah has the pleasure of our company, briefly.]

New Paddle

Ten months later, having forgotten about my aching hips and battered butt bones from February, I called Brian and we agreed to try the next 500 kilometres - the river would continue its north-westerly flow, heading up towards the top left-hand corner of Victoria. We would then be close to South Australia, deep in the Mallee country where not a lot of trees grow but hopefully the banks of the Murray would be dotted with some of our favourite river red gums.

In for a penny in for a pound as they say, or I may as well do the whole shebang, or whatever - I had decided to buy myself a new paddle. In the Coffs Harbour paper there was an advertisement for 'Mullaway Kayaks', they would be the people to visit to buy a new paddle. There I stared at a shed stuffed full of kayaks, and why I did not visit here four years ago I do not know. They could have sold me a faster kayak, something that would allowed me to row rings around Brian.

A charming lady asked me all the right questions: What type of kayak did I own? Was it a river or a sea kayak? Was it long or short? To make it easy I told her I was kayaking down the Murray River, in a long heavy plastic kayak with two storage holds. She guessed it was a Dagger Edisto - this woman knew her kayaks. She then asked me what sort of paddle I was after: Carbon fibre, fibre glass or graphite? Did I want it feathered or not? What off-set angle did I want? What length of paddle? By the blank look on my face, she quickly gained the impression that I did not know a lot about kayak paddles.

I explained that my plastic paddle came for free and that my kayaking partner says I should cut it into three hundred shower curtain rings. I think she was in step with Brian, telling me that to have a quality paddle was critical - I could paddle faster and with less effort. With that I was all ears. For some obscure reason she then asked me if I was left or right handed. Then she recommended I buy a feathered paddle, which (as she sternly told me), meant the blades would not be parallel but off-set to each other. With a gentle sigh of resignation she offered me some free advice:

"With kayaking, if you are right handed your right hand is your control hand and that raised part of the shaft on the right hand side is where your right hand grip is fixed. It does not change during the stroke. You can control the angle of the blade by your right hand. Your left hand should be holding the paddle shaft quite loosely and this allows your right hand to twist the paddle when you want to turn, or brace. Got that?"

163

So now I knew why my old plastic paddle had a raised part on the shaft, where I gripped it. I found that it was more comfortable with this on the right but I had no idea why it was there. I dare not tell her I had kayaked over a 1000 kilometres down the Murray without knowing all this.

She measured me, talked about 60 degree and 80 degree offsets with the paddles, mentioned $400 and smiled sweetly at me. A week later I was $400 dollars lighter but the owner of a new paddle.

I emailed Brian: 'Have new paddle. See you on the first of Feb.'

Returning to Swan Hill

On the last day of January in 2009 I kissed the hurry-home tear drops on Suzanne cheeks goodbye and left Coffs Harbour, on my 1400 kilometre drive to Swan Hill, this time through the back-blocks of NSW instead of down the Hume Highway. It was classic summer weather, varying from sultry at the peep of day, to a dog-day scorcher by noon, and remaining so even after the sun finally decided to wave a cheerio and drop out of sight in the evening. It had not rained for ages and I was worried that the Murray may have even less water and current than in past years.

I had brought along my iPod which, from experience, I found to be essential: one could go crazy listening to the radio, my choices being ABC or a local radio station when in a town. I tried ABC Radio National, where I heard the occasional interview that held my attention for a short while. However, gripping discussions giving 'an opportunity to hear the latest thinking on workplace safety', or debates on 'why America has lost its moral authority' soon lost me. These programs are for insomniacs - they are not designed to keep a driver awake. ABC News on the radio is like CNN news on TV - you can take a fifteen minute news bulletin once, or possibly twice in a

164

day - but no sane person can take it four times an hour, ten hours a day.

Within five kilometres of a town (of a reasonable size) I could pick up a local radio station but the drawback with these stations is twofold. First of all their reception radius is limited, starting at the 'Welcome to Armidale' sign as you enter the town and finishing at the 'you are leaving Armidale and thank you for not throwing beer bottles at our children' sign as you exit.

Secondly, these radio station announcers are usually lamentable, although not always. Parkes in Central New South Wales had a highly entertaining guy on as I drove through the town. He sounded like he was a grown up but his English was at the level of a five year old. "Ah. Dat song was for you by me. By de Kinks. Yeah, de Kinks. It was". He was real class, a true Australian red-neck hillbilly. Was he acting? I don't think so. He spoke like this for the whole ten minutes I took to drive through Parkes. I drove slowly to savour this guy and I was even tempted to turn around to listen some more after he disappeared off my radio radar, just as I passed the town exit sign, 'Thank you for visiting Parkes, home of the world's best radio announcers.'

After a night at Forbes, another small town out in the central-west of NSW, I was reliably informed by the announcer on Lauchlan Valley Community radio that the temperature was 36 degrees at seven in the morning; "fry an egg on the pavement" day, he called it. Forbes sits on the mighty Lauchlan River, hence the name of the radio station. I noticed the Lauchlan River was no longer so mighty, but a series of small muddy pools and dust bowls. This lack of water no doubt had a severe impact on the annual kayak race in Forbes, but on the positive side it put the kibosh on ever paddling down the Lauchlan with Brian.

Mitchell was on the lookout for the Lauchlan in the early days of his travels down to the Murray, in March 1836. He dropped

165

the 'u', calling it the Lachlan, and was keen to find it because he was certain he would find water in such a large river. However, the weather in 1836 seemed to be much like 2009: *'all the Lachlan's waters were gone, except in a few small ponds in the very deepest parts of its river bed.'*

At Swan Hill

But there I was, at Swan Hill, again, waiting for my old chum to arrive.

Oh, the joy of anticipation of it all! It was times like this that I wished an injury to Brian, so we had to give it all away. Nothing too serious I may add, just something like a small car crash which put him in hospital with a broken arm, leaving him unable to paddle. Or that he zapped himself fixing something electrical and burnt off all his body hair, so he looked like a half dead, half cooked seal, never able to ever go near water again.

But the bugger did arrive around mid-afternoon and we were, as always, pleased to see each other again. He was apologetic for being delayed: "Better late than never." The 'better late than never' words were his, not mine. He, as I expected, could not wait to get back on the river, although he was worried about the forecast for many hot days ahead, with possible total fire-ban days.

I showed him my new paddle.

"Wow! A Skee lightweight fibreglass one too. Wow! I bet this set you back a pretty penny. Why did you buy it now though? Why not wait until we are only a hundred kilometres from the end?"

I also showed him my new tent, one that rolls up to fit into a match-box; a larger than average match box. What I liked best about this new tent is it meant I would not have to stuff a sock in the rip that was in the bottom of my other tent, like I used to do every night. Brian had packed a water purifier so we could

166

'purify' some river water – he did not think the river water was now drinkable before boiling, or filtering. He had also brought along a new kayak seat which (so he told me) took him a week to put together. It looked very comfortable, like a lounge chair, sheep skin padded seat and it wrapped around both the seat and back rest of his kayak seat. Was I jealous? No. (That is a lie - you bet I was – the bastard!)

In 'Empty Quarter' heat at Swan Hill that afternoon, we pitched our tents in the camping ground and shopped for supplies at a supermarket, dawdling to delay venturing outside into the hot air.

('Empty Quarter' heat will only mean something if you have read *Desert Sands,* by Wilfred Thesiger. He is a loopy Englishman who joins up with a few Arab boys - he liked to travel with Arab boys – to travel across the Empty Quarter. In the southern desert of Arabia there is a large desert, bordered by Yemen, Oman and the coast: a desert within a desert. The Arabs call it the Empty Quarter. My hero Wilfred dresses as an Arab, hires a few camels, and don't forget the Arab boys, to trek across the desert. He writes an excellent book.)

At ten o'clock that night it still felt like somewhere between 35 and 40 degrees and sound sleep was hard to come by: something I badly needed if I was to at least start off this journey in good spirit. A few early rising chooks interrupted the morning's peace and quiet, with a little cock-a-doodling, followed by the chorus of wild spirits of our old friends the kookaburras, (I told you I liked that phrase). Finally the sun popped its head up over the trees and looked left, looked right, looked left again and then said: 'There's a place that needs warming up; the Swan Hill camping ground', before pumping some hot air in our direction.

On his travels back in the 1830's, Sturt occasionally waxed lyrical about the weather, preferring southern NSW to the *'intolerable'* weather in India, where the man was born.

He tells us that one '*may cast himself at length under the first tree that invites him, and repose there as safely as if he were in a* palace' and wake up '*unmolested by noxious insects... he rises with renewed spirits to pursue his journey.*'

He even had a view on how the '*coolness of the morning and the mild temperature of the evening air*' might have a '*happy effect upon some of the hardened human beings who are sent thither from the old world.*' (In other words, all the convicts sent to Australia would end up cheery good natured souls.)

Another Day 1

There was no 'coolness of the morning' for Brian and I, simply another scorching summers day, although as two 'hardened human beings' we spent much of the day in our air-conditioned cars, dropping one at Mildura, and then driving back to Swan Hill. Eventually we were ready, standing by our kayaks, gazing at the river, delaying the start - I felt we needed a starter's gun to get us moving. It was 522 river kilometres to Mildura, which should be a doddle for me now I had my new paddle. I even thought I might have to slow down to allow Brian to keep up.

By the map book we were to head north, then west, then north again, passing a town called Nyah, then a day or two later we should see another town Tooleybuc. Then the mighty Murrumbidgee River was to come in from the north, 180 kilometres away - four or five days paddling. It was there we would join up with Sturt, and be paddling on the same waters he did in 1830, all the way down to the sea (hopefully).

For some time after the Murrumbidgee junction there was not much in the way of a shack or a shanty, let alone a village of any sorts, until the town of Robinvale. Uh-oh! I then spotted a bloody lock after Robinvale, Lock number 15. I wondered what happened to all the locks between Robinvale and Torrumbarry, as it was Lock 26 at Torrumbarry. My guess is that a fellow kayaker blew them up, and I hoped someone had

168

done the same to the fourteen locks after Lock 15. After Robinvale we were to pass the '1000 kilometres to the end of the river' sign, which was sort of significant, and then we would hit Mildura, at the 888 marker (after seeing Brian's World's Biggest Red Gum Tree, a day or two before reaching Mildura). This leg should be a doddle, or so I thought.

It was five o'clock before we were on the river and for a change there were a few people scattered about in the water and on the banks, as we drifted down through the outskirts of Swan Hill. Like the wallabies of a year ago they had come down to the river to cool themselves and we remarked how friendly the people were as they kept saying hello.

We passed a grey curly haired elderly lady with her feet up on a log. Next to her was her fast-asleep husband, at least I presumed he was asleep, not dead. She did not look like a killer but you never know these days. She may have been waiting for us to go by before giving the old guy a nudge with her toe, sending him rolling down the bank into the river. I saw no concrete blocks tied to his boots though, so he was probably asleep.

We saw blue-singlet-wearing young bucks and their smudged mascara-eyed girls sitting in utes backed down to the river, with the rear wheels in the water and tail gate down. They waved a can of beer in our direction and yelled out: "Hey guys, feel like a beer?"

After a couple of hours of easy paddling we camped, having travelled a mammoth 10 kilometres and what better way to celebrate having travelled 10 kilometres than to enjoy the finest in Irish beverages, a can of Guinness, chilled courtesy of ice we had bought at Swan Hill? My hero Thesiger did not carry cans of Gunness and at times he had real water problems going across the desert in Arabia, as you can well imagine. They had a small goatskin full of milk which they would '*mix a little everyday with our drinking water and that would improve its taste.*'

169

Apparently, this is the way the Arabs who live in the desert make their water drinkable. Thesiger tells us that they '*call this mixture of sour milk and water shanin.*'

The Swan Hill wind decided it needed to lie low and didn't move all night, except just before dawn when it shuffled in its sleep and a wee breeze sprang up. Our morning coolish breeze did not last long and by seven in the morning it changed to a strong warm wind from the north-east. The day felt summery, even at that early hour.

We had camped near the '1398 kilometres to the end of the river' sign and coming up I could see a 'mud bank' marked, then some 'clay showing' after an hour possibly, then 'grass growing' on our left after the 1392 marker. Now if we had wanted a geography lesson all of this detail would be fascinating - but how was it relevant to a couple of kayakers? I noticed we would pass something called a Takasuka Monument, dedicated to a Jo Takasuka who, so the map book told me, came here from Japan in 1905 to start the first rice crop. There was no need for us to stop and view the Takasuka Monument.

Off we went, finding it cooler on the river and especially cooler for me because even with my new paddle, I still managed to drop water on myself. I did not notice any significant improvement in my paddling speed though; possibly it would take me a day or two to get the hang of it. The water drops were a blessing because at ten in the morning the day had the hallmarks of a scorcher. We noticed far more wildlife down by the river than we ever had before, black wallabies, kangaroos, wild looking dogs, feral cats and a few emus. We guessed they were down by the river for a drink, and to cool down.

These sorts of sights make the whole trip worthwhile for Brian. He loved seeing native animals.

"Look at those wood ducks. See how one of them is pretending to be lame and is half-flying half-splashing along in front of us to lead us away from his nest or his babies."

"Did you see those couple of pelicans?"

"Look at that magnificent red kangaroo over there," he whispered.

Mitchell, in June 1836, when following the Murray up from the Darling past this point to Swan Hill, enjoyed seeing the wildlife as much as Brian, making one note that the "*country abounded with kangaroos*". He was most delighted when he discovered an unusual animal:

This animal was of the size of a young wild rabbit and of nearly the same colour, but had a broad head terminating in a long very slender snout, like the narrow neck of a wide bottle; and it had no tail.

The forefeet were singularly formed, resembling those of a hog; and the marsupial opening was downwards, and not upwards as in the kangaroo and others of that class of animals.

(Any guesses as to what it was? My environmentalist buddy Brian would not have known either. It was a Pig-footed Bandicoot, a *Chaeropus ecaudatus*, a small marsupial – so Mitchell's journal notes tell me.)

Nyah

By mid- afternoon we had reached Nyah, with the map showing another town called Nyah West just a few kilometres away inland. We parked our kayaks, and, in a searing heat that dried our wet hats in a few seconds, we walked up to the dried-out town of Nyah; which has not a lot going for it when the temperature is in the low 40's and there is a howling hot wind roaring down the main street.

Well may you may ask why there are two Nyah towns, stuck out here in north east Victoria. Apparently Nyah, which is right on the river, was formed in the late 1800s as some sort of a socialist community, whereas Nyah West is on a railway line, a line most inconveniently built a few kilometres away from Nyah. Nyah West is claimed to be the most complete 1920's style town in Victoria - full of art deco – with more old world charm than Nyah. Having visited Nyah that day I would say that it's not difficult to have more old-word charm than Nyah.

After Nyah we pushed on with Brian setting the pace and me struggling to keep up – so much for this new $400 paddle making any difference. The slice of my brain that creates excitement cells, or motivation, or drive, or even just the prod to paddle had gone to sleep or died in Nyah. Brian, fine man that he is, did his best to cajole me along, chit-chatting away on topics like the circumference of women's thighs, a topic which always kept me alert.

We stopped for a stretch, clambering up the dusty river bank to see what could be of interest near the river, but there was

172

nothing; just dry bush land of struggling gum trees on sandy soil, for as far as we could see. We stood there and looked at the bush, saying nothing, and the bush looked back at us, also saying nothing. It was so silent and so still. Brian told me a phrase teachers like to holler at their class is: "I want to hear silence!" But you cannot ever hear silence, can you?

Chapter 15: 'romantic-looking scene'

[Our stop at Tooleybuc is also brief. A significant milestone, we see the sign, 1250 kilometres to the sea – halfway! We close in on the junction with the Murrumbidgee.]

Water filtering

That night we camped next to the 1348 distance marker, a dry dusty spot with limited shade from a few gnarled gum trees. Brian spent time in the water, progressing through a range of activities: shampooing his hair, washing his clothes and trying out the water purifier. We had to use the purifier as we couldn't light a fire to boil up water - it was a total fire ban day – as Brian informed me after listening to the news on his radio. We sure did not want to be the clowns who set fire to the bush, which started a fire storm that wiped out Nyah.

This purifier consisted of a couple of hoses, a hand pump and a container. It worked by filling the container with river water, which we then had to pump out the top outlet through a filter, and into our water bottles. Brian called me into the water to help and there we were; both of us butt naked, up to our goolies in the water. I was holding an empty two litre water bottle between my knees and holding in the hoses at the bottle and purifier ends, Brian was pumping the purifier to force water through the filter.

"Now, it is times like these," I commented, "that those two elusive Swedish backpackers will come around the corner and keep paddling on past because here we are, naked as a couple of jaybirds, carrying out an activity that would appear highly questionable to say the least."

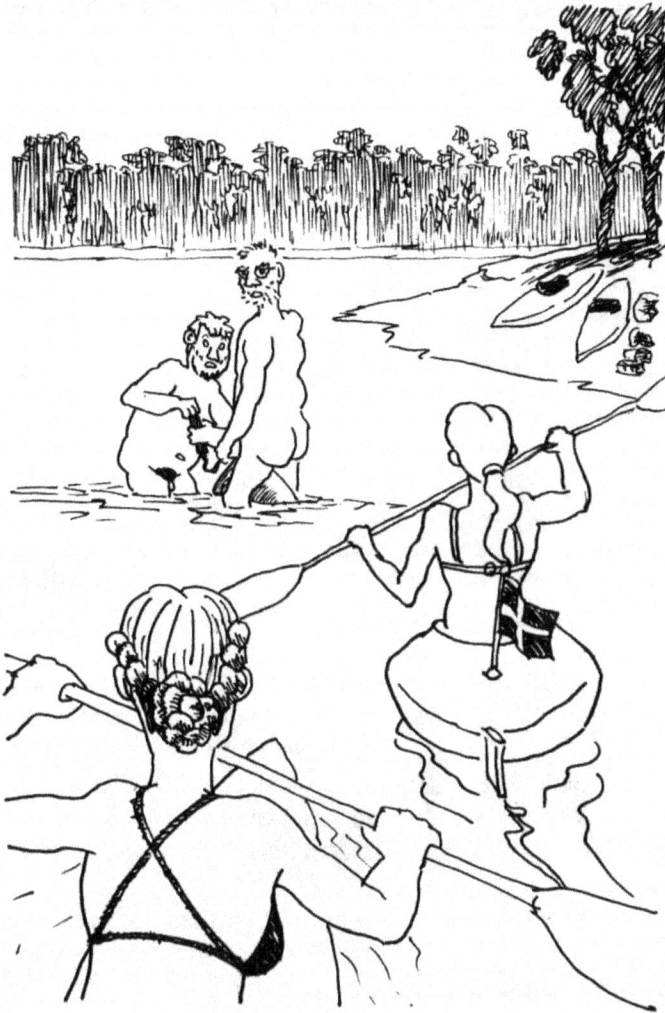

Just a side note: of interest to those who have been noticing the occasional mention of Swedish backpackers, it was not Swedish but Amazon women who were uppermost in the minds of early explorers, well uppermost in Hovell's mind anyway. After he and Hume had battled their way through the bush one day Hovell wrote that it was impossible to describe the brush or scrub, being worse than '*any jungle in any other country*'.

He added:

Mr. Hume had his face so nearly covered with the brambles and boyers that it appeared as if it had been done by the fair hand of some Amazonian damsel;

Hot days

Brian heard on his radio the next morning that we were in for yet another total fire ban day. The forecast was for a stinker weather-wise, and for the next few days too; with hot northerly winds and exceedingly high temperatures. A forecast like that brought us no joy because we would be heading generally north-west from here to Mildura, although now and again it would loop back a little and do a waggle to the west, to the south or even east, but generally it weaved north-west.

In oven-hot air and into a baking blustery wind we slogged away, dunking our head-gear regularly. Every hour of paddling was followed by a swim and a walk up to the top of the river bank, hoping to see something of interest – without success. At times we donned our David Attenborough hats to study a few ants or a bird track, to delay the inevitable.

On the river we could see nothing other than the bank and the first line or two of trees because of the low water level. The map book showed nothing nearby, just a town called Tooleybuc, which we would pass tomorrow.

Bitch and pups

"Tooleybuc, Tooleybuc, here we are in Tooleybuc", I sang to myself, in a good mood because we had planned to stop here for the night and that meant I had no more paddling for the day. But Tooleybuc met us on a bad day – we didn't feel like hauling our kayaks up a steep bank across to the caravan park,

176

and so we pushed on, and Tooleybuc missed out on the pleasure of our company.

Back on the river it was slightly cooler than it was on the Tooleybuc concrete footpath and we coasted along in slow motion, in a sort of first gear paddling mode. The wind was insistent, dirty and suffocating, but it was even more unpleasant when we stopped for a break: on the river bank the sand and dry dust squalled all around us.

We camped late, moaning and groaning about the heat, and justifiably as it was still oppressively hot. The only bonus for the day was that we had seen even more animals by the river - wild pigs, wallabies, emu, even sheep and cows - flocks of sheep and heaps of cows, or herds of cows if you must be pedantic.

At the place we had stopped there was a little island in the middle of the river. I studied the map book and it showed the island plus two smaller islands nearby too.

"Patrick, guess the name of that island and the two other smaller ones."

"Is this quiz time?" he asked. 'Do I get to ask you a question in return?"

"The three islands are called Bitch and pups. Pretty smart eh? Bitch and two pups. Big island and two small ones."

Understandably Brian had no interest in this bit of river trivia. He was listening to his radio, worried about bush fires around his house in the Indigo Valley.

Mitchell saw the same islands back in 1836. Riding along, following the course of the river, 'we came upon a most romantic-looking scene where a flood branch had left a serpentine piece of water, enclosing two wooded island.'

Mitchell was also impressed by the trees, and he wrote that they *'passed through forests of the box or goborro' and that he saw 'yarra trees also.'*

A lateral thinker was our Mitchell, noting also that the area *'seemed very favourable for farms or cattle stations'* and that the land *'seemed capable of being converted into good wheat land, and of being easily irrigated at any time by the river.'*

(And of course Mitchell was proven to be spot on with his forecast, as these days you can find a cluster of cattle men or wheat farmers on almost every corner of Tooleybuc, a town Brian and I were due to meet very soon.)

Half way

The wind Gods were in a mongrel mood the next day, with the fiery wind continuing, and still from the north. I scanned the map book at a rest stop, hoping for another short cut like we had on the first day, preferably one direct to Mildura. The Wakool River came in 18 kilometres on from where we had camped so we hoped a strong river flow would be joining the Murray to help us along, but the Wakool had shrivelled up into a pithy little creek, with no water flowing in to help us.

The river wobbled along, heading west before turning to loop back on itself, which showed that if we were on horseback like Mitchell we could have cut many a corner. Our 'scenic' view from the kayaks varied occasionally when we passed by rock shelves and 20 to 30 metre high cliffs along the river's edge, but these did not interest us a great deal.

Passing the 1250 distance marker late in the afternoon did interest us. We stopped and cheered as we had made the halfway point and no better reason to camp I thought, so we did. We looked around for a big signpost saying 'Wilson & Brian, you are halfway from the source of the Murray to the mouth. Well done old chaps' but our only company was a dusty piece of ground for us to put our tents on and five scraggly scruffy gum trees behind us.

The junction of the Murray with the Murrumbidgee was only eight kilometres away and I had high hopes that meeting the Murrumbidgee might be a life-changer for me, a sort of born again experience. I was expecting that after the junction I'd be able to sit back and just go with the water flow. Would there be huge volumes of water coming down the Murrumbidgee; such a torrent as to double the speed of the Murray? Would I be able to then surf the waves all the way down to Goolwa?

Chapter 16: 'on the high road'

[The Murrumbidgee brings us no joy. The weather deteriorates into a 'Black Saturday'. Robinvale is in our sights.]

We meet the Murrumbidgee

On the 6th of February 2009 the McOrist – Rock pair of merry men were boating down the Murray and they reached the junction of the mighty Murrumbidgee; but Murrumbidgee was mighty no longer, quite the opposite: it looked close to stagnant. Gallons of water weren't being pumped into *our* Murray, far from it.

"I don't believe it!" Brian exclaimed. "At best the Murrumbidgee is now just a creek, if not a piddling little inlet. It's hard to tell if water is even flowing out of it. Quite possibly water is even flowing back up the Murrumbidgee."

Over 170 years ago, on the 14th of January 1830 Sturt and his band of merry men were boating down the Murrumbidgee when they noticed a change in its flow, that made them believe the Murrumbidgee was about to end, and they were right. Sturt wrote:

... the singular change in the river had impressed ... that we were approaching its termination, or near some adventure. On a sudden, the river took a general southern direction, but, in its tortuous course, swept round to every point of the compass with the greatest irregularity.

At 3 p.m., Hopkinson called out that we were approaching a junction, and in less than a minute afterwards, we were hurried into a broad and noble river.

Sturt goes on to describe meeting the Murray and he is obviously tickled pink. (Remember, it was not yet called the

Murray, it was still the 'Hume' – he is to re-name it the Murray a week later.)

It is impossible for me to describe the effect of so instantaneous a change of circumstances upon us.

The boats were allowed to drift along at pleasure, and such was the force with which we had been shot out of the Morumbidgee, that we were carried nearly to the bank opposite its embouchure.

Having reached the Murray, Sturt now believed he was on track to reach the southern ocean. He was a smart cookie and he now guessed (correctly) that other rivers had joined the Murray further upstream:

We had got on the high road, as it were, either to the south coast, or to some important outlet; I could not doubt its being the great channel of the streams from the S.E. angle of the island. Mr. Hume had mentioned to me that he crossed three very considerable streams, when employed with Mr. Hovell in 1823 in penetrating towards Port Phillips, to which the names of the Goulburn, the Hume, and the Ovens, had been given.

After the Murrumbidgee junction

The water speed of the Murray did not change at all for us after the Murrumbidgee junction, it felt like the same slow-moving 'Old Man Murray River'. We cursed the heat, gave the hot wind a good old tongue lashing, and called down on all rice and cotton growers who we believed drained the rivers of its waters. We poured vitriol on everyone and anyone we happened to think of.

Our map book told us there was a general store coming up soon, at Boundary Bend, where we hoped to buy a meat pie and a 44 gallon drum of ice cold water. I mentioned this to Brian – big mistake. He upped his stroking rate considerably at

181

the thought of a meat pie, and I was left to roll along on my own for a couple of hours, with Brian just a speck on the river way ahead, mostly keeping to the centre of the river but occasionally suddenly shooting across to the bank for some obscure reason. A familiar sight.

Boundary Bend was an oasis, at least it was for two hot, hungry, dehydrated guys who walked into the only store in town - a service station - finding fish and chips for sale and a fridge full of cold drinks.

"May the Lord bless Boundary Bend" I said to Brian.

"Amen," he replied, croaking out an order for two plates of fish and chips and 200 cans of drink.

We pushed on. Brian listened to his radio intently as there was news on a number of bush fires in southern Victoria, while I listened to the sound of my paddle sloshing in and out of the water. I thought of a little known Australian explorer called Dick Richards. He was a member of an expedition to the Antarctic way back, in 1915, and his role was to man-haul sledges of provisions for Shackleton. This took weeks and weeks of monotonous sledge hauling across the Antarctic Great Ice Barrier, so he used to do mathematical calculations in his head to help pass the time.

I tried doing the same. Okay, I told myself, you have just passed the 1224 distance marker, so it is two kilometres to the next. If you do one paddle stroke a second and it takes you 20 minutes to do two kilometres, how many paddle strokes do you need? I had no idea. It was all too hard a row to hoe, or a river to row, so I switched off, put my mind into cruise-control and flopped the arms over and over until I caught up with Brian, which happened only when he had to stop for a wee.

We felt quite alone up in the back blocks north west Victoria (or south west NSW if you prefer), with the service station back at Boundary Bend our last sign of people and the

182

township of Robinvale still a few days ahead. Not that it worried us in the slightest. Brian had his radio to listen to, and I had Brian to listen to. He told me that the Australian Open tennis had been cancelled for the next day (Saturday) and it was forecast to be 46 degrees in Melbourne with winds up to eighty kilometres an hour. They advised everyone to stay out of the heat, to stay indoors and keep cool. Well I was in favour of that in theory, now all I needed was a suggestion or two on where in this neck of the woods some 'doors' would pop up so we could go 'indoors' and keep cool.

Black Saturday

The next day, Saturday, was foul. Even in the early morning a noisy ill-wind howled around us; a wind as dry as dust; sounding like a freight train and coming from the centre of the country. The sky too had a sinister look, dirty and dusty, grey and hazy. It would be a terrible day for paddling because the river headed north-west so with a northerly wind it would be tough, but it was too uncomfortable at the camp site so we decided to get on the river and do what we could.

Off we went; water bottles between our knees and sun-blocked to the hilt. The wind intensified and became stronger - by mid-morning it felt like a gale, and a burning hot gale at that. It was sometimes into our faces, sometimes across the river, and occasionally behind us, pushing us along when we had a stretch of the river going south. At times we would shelter by the edge to have a rest and if the river turned at the next corner into the wind we would steel ourselves for a hard slog. Round the bend we would go and the wind would hit us. Bang! Then it was head down and teeth gritted, paddling like fury to move forward.

We could not travel in the middle of the river, the wind was too strong and the waves were too high, so we had to inch our way along by the bank. If we stopped for a second, the wind blew us backwards against the current. When the river changed direction the side with shelter would change too, so we would have to cross the river, battling through a mass of white caps, and I went close to flipping a few times. After a few hours I felt all-in and dead-beat with sore arm muscles. Our progress wasn't satisfactory, but there was not a lot we could do but laugh at it all.

"Great fun, eh?" I said to Brian, as we hung onto a couple of logs to avoid being pushed back upstream.

"This is what it's all about McOrist. Any bugger can paddle down a river, but this is a real challenge. This is what makes men of us. Let's go."

He was as happy as Larry, whoever Larry was - perhaps a larrikin who liked to lark about. Tosser I thought (not Larry, Brian), no one could enjoy this, but I had no one to hear my grumbles and grousing over the wind, so off I went again. This ordeal went on all day and we found the best way to handle it was to break the day down into stages, a short stretch of water at a time, then a rest, then another hard paddle, then a rest. Our only company was wild life, foxes and wild pigs now joining the emus and wallabies by the river, and many birds, such as pelicans, swans and ducks by the dozen who opted to stay in the water rather than flying around.

184

We kept paddling until late in the evening because to stop early would be too unpleasant. At seven thirty it started to become quite gloomy, due in part to the dust and haze in the air which cut out a lot of the sunlight. We camped and I lay on the ground feeling parched and horribly sun-dried.

Brian was still giving me bushfire updates. There were bushfires in and around the township of Marysville, but no reports of any serious ones up near his place, yet.

Then later on he said: "Reports now of six people dead in the Kinglake area."

It kept getting worse: "Fourteen dead now, and fires near my home at Beechworth."

This brought my kayaking day back into perspective. I went to bed not feeling so whacked out and dog-tired.

Were we finished?

By the following morning the weather had broken - the wind gods had decided it was time for a breather. The temperature had dropped considerably but the sky was still hazy, a grey, smoky, murky look. The sun was up there – we could see it behind the haze.

The bush fire reports coming in on Brian's radio sobered us up. The Beechworth fires were not close to his house, but many houses in Marysville and Kinglake were gone although they said everyone in Marysville was safe. We thought we should get to Robinvale late today and Brian could call his dear lady Trish - he may have to go back home and look after her.

We had 40 kilometres to Robinvale, but there was a possible, potential, promising, on the cards, hunky-dory snippet of news for us - there looked like a short cut that could shave ten kilometres off our travels. The good map book showed a cutting, called Bumbang Cutting, but it needed sufficient water to cover a clay bridge in the cutting to be open as a short cut.

We heard more reports of the bush fire - with over 90 now confirmed dead and Marysville burnt to the ground. Paddling did not seem drudgery anymore.

After lunch we came to a fork in the river and for many boats there would have been insufficient water depth, but we managed to pull ourselves through the Bumbang Cutting, in some places with nothing but river weed on the surface of a few inches of water. Saving those ten kilometres beat almost everything; but not quite the sight of the girl's breasts in Barham.

Bar is Open

A few kilometres out from Robinvale we passed some guys fishing out of a small square motor boat with a canopy on top, with a 'Bar is Open' sign displayed on the side.

They explained to us that their bar never shuts, and asked where we were heading for. We explained:

"All the way. The Full Monty."

"Hey good luck. We're only doing the stretch from Echuca to Robinvale this year. Last year we did Yarrawonga to Echuca. We meet every year with this boat, stock it up with beer and food and travel a few hundred kilometres at a time, fishing and drinking."

These guys approached river travel differently to Brian and me. They used a putt-putt motor to push themselves along; they carried beer, ice and probably a stash of quality food. They were on holiday. However Brian and I agreed, almost sincerely, that we were not jealous of their soft city-slickers approach. We were happy to be kayaking. Even though at this time I had began to feel how hard and painful paddling had become, as though the water flow had ceased. It was like we were in a lake, rather than on a river with current. A putt-putt motor would have helped.

At a rest spot I saw that Robinvale was only five kilometres ahead and a lock five kilometres further on – so that was the reason for the lack of water flow.

At the Robinvale camping ground Brian called Trish and his house was not under immediate threat or any threat at all; so Trish said there no need to stop, we could go on; bugger it.

Saturday February 7th 2009 became known as "Black Saturday". Over 400 fires were recorded across Victoria and there were 78 communities affected. 173 people lost their lives and 2029 homes were destroyed. South-eastern Australia had been affected by an extreme heat wave in late January and early February 2009 and there were twelve consecutive days with temperatures of above 40°C at Mildura.

On that day a temperature of 48.8°C was recorded in north-east Victoria, (a Victorian state record) and the highest temperature ever recorded in the world so far south of the equator. A Royal Commission was established to investigate the cause of the bushfires and found that the majority of the fires were started by fallen or clashing power lines, or were deliberately lit. A drought had persisted for more than 10 years which facilitated burning.

Chapter 17: 'on the alert to kill'

[The weather cools. The sea is less than 1000 kilometres away. We are on the lookout for snakes but we miss the Big Gum Tree.]

Asians on Sunday

There is but one bright light of Robinvale, an Asian goods general store. It had a roaring trade going for a hot lazy Sunday afternoon, selling everything from umbrellas to noodles, coriander, camping chairs, internet access, surf boards, chocolate eggs, garden gnomes, tyre jacks, lamp shades and even DVD's of Pamela Anderson.

After a week on the river we craved a few cold beers and a thick chunk of the finest beef this Mallee region could produce, followed by a few more beers. But if you are after a Sunday pub meal of steak and chips, don't hold on for Robinvale. We asked the bar girl what time the meals came on but she stopped us in our tracks - there were no meals today, it was a Sunday. This was a message that two steak-starved kayakers did not want to hear. We were shattered. So much so we only had two beers, watching a few toothless tattooed locals watching us before we left and had a Chinese meal. The Chinese work on Sundays in Robinvale.

We got under way from Robinvale early the next morning, refreshed and replenished, clean in body if not in mind, and with Brian's kayak full of clean clothes. An hour down the track we met Lock 15 at Euston Weir and we could see the water level below the lock was lower. The map book gave us a phone number, so we phoned the lock-man to let us through and let us through he did. We drifted into the lock bay; the lock-man closed the huge back doors behind us, lowered the water level in the lock by pumping water out, opened the huge front doors and bugger me; we were at the level of the river below the lock.

I had just seen the perfect job for someone who wanted an easy life. That man would never have any worries, stress or concerns. A few times a day he turns a couple of knobs to let cheerful guys like us through and the rest of the day he just sits there, perhaps counting the rivets on the lock doors and watching Pamela Anderson DVD's, but more likely keeping accurate graphs on water levels and fish movements.

After the lock the water flowed once again, not a rushing torrent but a little flow to make us feel better, which in truth meant we travelled about five kilometres an hour instead of four. We had a light cool southerly wind and the river headed chiefly in a southerly direction (for a change) so paddling was a pleasure, especially when we passed by some captivating red cliffs. We even paused and looked at them, which was a rarity for me, to stop and look at anything other than a blue marker.

The next evening, after a 48 kilometre paddling day, my body was not happy, I was sore; my wrists and knees and feet in particular – it was my old man's arthritis Brian told me – but I thought I should be as tough as nails now with all this exercise. Unlike me Brian felt fine - his arms were sore for the first couple of days but now he reckoned he could go on and on, past Mildura and all the way, if I liked. I did not like.

Less than 1000 to go

In the bush at night we saw and heard no-one, apart from the dulcet tones of Peter Roebuck commentating on a night cricket game, interspersed with reports on the bush fire calamity. My eyes were glued to the map book, looking for and finding some good news; possible short cuts on the next day. I saw we would be passing a place called Retail Cutting which was a new formation of the river cutting off eight kilometres, then there was a Doherty's Bend with a small short cut that would take off two kilometres off, and finally, at a spot called Tarpaulin Cutting, the old river was silted up and we would go from the 1008 marker straight to the 1000 marker, a saving of another eight kilometres.

190

Brian forgot the cricket for a minute. "Forget a few kilometres saved. Do you know what you are saying? Tomorrow we get below the 1000 kilometre mark? That is a huge milestone."

We blessed Mr and Mrs Doherty for their bend which saved us two kilometres, had even more praise for Mr and Mrs Retail for their cutting that saved us eight kilometres and boy did we ever holler long and loud to Mr and Mrs Tarpaulin for silting up eight kilometres of the old river. We had saved 18 kilometres in total. I thought all my birthdays had come at once.

The map book now showed a lot of pumps, and we started to see them, huge water pipes pumping water out of the river; sets of four pipes, five pipes and even nine pipes at a time. We were amazed there was any water left in the Murray, or the Murrumbidgee if it comes to that. We did not take kindly to pumps sucking water out of our rivers.

We stopped for a rest where the map book showed the 1000 sign but some bastard had nicked it, as likely as not a kayaker, so we went on, stopping for our next rest near the 994 blue marker and taking a photo of this highly significant occasion.

You may think I exaggerate our delight in passing from four digit blue marker numbers to three digit ones, but you know by now I am not one to exaggerate. I may stretch the truth a tad about Brian's undies scrubbing and hair shampooing but we really did feel over the moon on seeing a three digit number on a blue sign. Not that we did a hop-scotch or the hula-hula, but we did give out a loud "Yes!"

We had passed Mount Dispersion, which surprised me as I thought there were no mountains in this part of the country - it is a flat as a pancake. The map book stated the hill was named by Major Mitchell after he apparently dispersed a bunch of aborigines - an incident in which seven of them were shot dead.

Mitchell wrote in his journal that '*a vast body of blacks (were) following our track, shouting prodigiously, and raising war cries.*'

He was unsure if they were really hostile so he had half of his men hide and wait but the aborigines spotted the ambush, '*by the howling of one of their dogs, halted and poised their spears.*'

One of Mitchell's men took umbrage at this and started '*discharging his carabine.*' The other half of Mitchell's men heard the shooting and '*ran furiously down the steep bank to the river*' joining in the shooting at the aborigines, now swimming across the river.

Mitchell '*regretted the necessity for firing upon these savages*' but he believed that '*they were on the alert to kill*' his men.

He then named the little hill '*which witnessed this overthrow of our enemies ... the name of Mount Dispersion.*'

This incident did not go down too well at the time, and an inquest held later found that one of Mitchell's men had fired before any order was given. The Sydney Morning Herald of January 27 1837 reported the evidence of Mitchell's right hand man, who stated:

One of the men of my party fired a shot at them, the blacks all took the river and were crossing the river when we fired, then we never saw any more of them.

In 1830, six years before Mitchell, Sturt also ran into '*a large body of natives*' on this part of the Murray. Unlike Mitchell's men, Sturt and his men kept their cool and decided against ripping a brace of bullets into the locals. Sturt was a man for negotiation and mediation, none of this 'shoot first, ask questions after' approach.

He talked to them, across the river, no doubt displaying some classic charade moves - in Sturt's words": '*I held a long pantomimical dialogue with them, across the water.*'

But Sturt got his message across - a few of the aborigines '*laid aside their spears*' and joined him. Sturt was fascinated, as an Englishman would be on seeing aboriginals in the bush in 1830. He gave, as was his custom,' *the first who had approached, a tomahawk; and to the others, some pieces of iron hoop.*'

Snake camp

The next day, by virtue of twelve hours of paddling, we had covered close to 52 kilometres, and we camped by the 968 blue marker. Brian did not like the reeds and some big logs nearby as he though it made for snake country. He suggested moving on, but it was late, and with tired bodies and hungry stomachs we had reached the end of the day for paddling.

"Come here my friend and have a look at this," Brian called out.

There between our tents, our kayaks, and items spread around were lines in the sand - snake tracks, and there were lots of them. They went from the reeds, through our camp site, down to the logs by the river, and back again. Brian suggested we move on, but this would have meant pulling down the tents, packing all our bits and pieces back in the kayaks, and trying to find another spot, all before it got completely dark.

"We will be okay," I said. "There is an old bush trick to stop snakes coming into a camp site and that is to piss all around the tents. They will never cross a piss line."

Thank God he believed me. It was the best story I could make up on the spot, to save from moving on.

Brian did not dawdle around the next morning, for all I know he may have been walking around all night with his head light on, looking for snakes. For the first time ever he was up and ready to go before me. He was first down with his tent, first to pack up his kayak and first on the water.

"Come on slow coach. Let's get this show on the road. Every day it's the same. Here I am sitting in my kayak waiting and waiting for you to get ready."

Problem: Brian is slow to get moving in the mornings.
Solution: Make snake tracks in sand.

The Big Gum Tree

At our first rest stop for the day I read a note on the page in the map book: 'Sign 'Big Red Gum Tree 60m'. This tree is reputed to be the biggest red gum in NSW and probably the world'. We were there! Brian had mentioned that he wanted to see this tree, and have his photo taken leaning against it. Here we were, finally at the place of the big tree.

I then noticed we had a small problem. The tree was by the 968 distance marker, six kilometres back – exactly where we had camped last night! I did not see the note before we got there, or before we left. I could not believe it. We may have even slept under it. Should I tell Brian? I thought it was best not to.

I did mention to him that today we would be travelling through the Mallee Cliffs State Forest and then the famous Red Cliffs (I used the word famous advisedly in that not many people outside Victoria know of these cliffs). So, we could expect to see some cliffs that were red. I hoped this would keep his mind off any big gum trees, and it did. We made the cliffs, and we agreed they were quite impressive, even to a weary old paddler like me. We drifted slowly alongside them - some 50-70 metre high and all with bright red soil, perpendicular and with their summits perfectly level.

The river was slowly widening, and with that, the current diminishing; not that it slowed Brian down as he happily stroked along, cutting across the river at times to look at a hole in the cliff, or to check out suitable hourly-resting places. The cliffs made it difficult to stop so we pushed on. I was now

195

dropping well back, with Brian stopping and waiting for me, shouting some encouraging words or staying with me for a while to try to cheer me up with some witty remarks, usually about teachers (who have little to do during school recess than tell teacher jokes in the staff room, apparently). At one time we resorted to 'I Spy' - yes, grown up men do play 'I Spy' - which whittled away an hour or so, and took my mind off my aches and pains.

By evening Mildura was only thirty-two kilometres away and we camped in the Gol Gol State Forest. Gol Gol. What a great name! Like Wagga Wagga, Grong Grong, Woy Woy, Mitta Mitta and dozens of other places around Australia it's doubled barrelled. Wagga is supposed to come from the Wiradjuri aboriginal name for crow and to create the plural, the Wiradjuri people repeated the word – hence Wagga Wagga is the place of many crows. There is some doubt about this crow claim, however. Some people now refer to 'waggawagga' as meaning 'dancing' or 'staggering like a drunken man' – a typical early description of an Indigenous corroboree by early English settlers only familiar with the waltz, or possibly Jane Austin's description in *Northanger Abbey*: '*People that dance, only stand opposite each other in a long room for half an hour.*'

By the way, Gol Gol got its name from the local Aboriginal term for 'meeting place', as our good friend Mitchell recorded in 1836. So there may be many good meeting places at Gol Gol - but we were not stopping to check them out.

Enough is enough

Our final plod the next day into Mildura was just that; the plod, plod, plod of my paddle dropping into the water. I read somewhere that this is called tea-bag dipping, where there is no effort put into each stroke, just the dipping of the paddle into the water. Instead of Mallee scrub or red cliffs lining the edge of the river we started to see houseboats and willows. In fact, as we neared Mildura we could see nothing but houseboats and willows. Some of them were huge, like floating 10 bedroom mansions, and some were small, like a packing case on four 44 gallon drums. Does anyone in Mildura live on land, I wondered, or do they all live on houseboats on the river?

By lunchtime we only had 16 kilometres to go which would be four hours paddling and I could handle that. I paddled along keeping close to the edge by the houseboats, hoping to glimpse a kayak transport truck on the lookout for customers, and also to keep away from speedboats, in the middle of the river.

At mid-afternoon we beached at the Buronga Caravan Park, over the river from the Mildura township. Brian looked at me. The man was a mind reader.

"You don't want to continue on, do you?" I shook my head.

He went on: "Next year we can start again from here, and we may even get to the finish." I shook my head when he wasn't looking.

"And next year we must make sure we see that big gum tree," Brian added. "It must be after Mildura. Check the map before we start next year so we don't miss it."

STAGE 5:

2011. Finally, it's all over

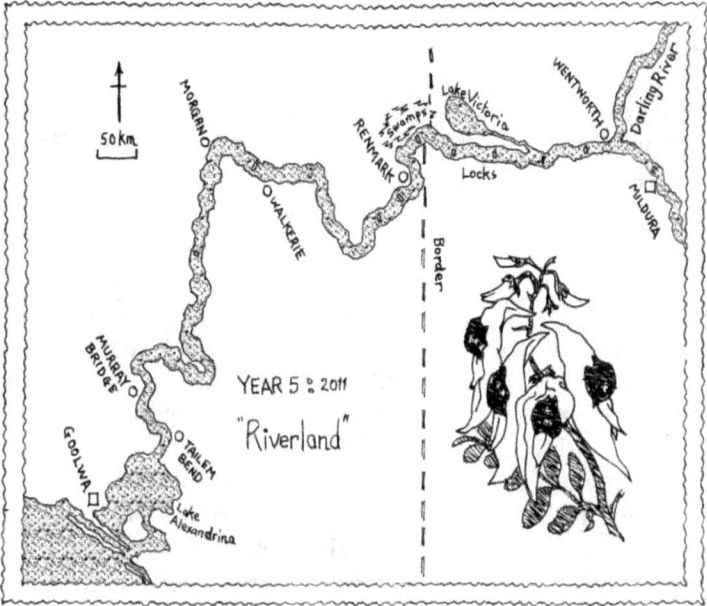

Chapter 18: 'a beautiful stream'

[We do not paddle in 2010. Severe flooding does not deter us and we meet in February 2011. The river carries us along at great rate. We camp by Sturt's tree at Wentworth.]

Our plans to finish

In the following year I suggested to Brian, that to stand the best chance of finishing, we should leave one car near Goolwa at the end of the river. I would have no choice then but to continue all the way - no more quitting for me. That was fine by him.

The map book showed that we had **888** kilometres from Mildura to the end, passing through Lock 11, with the first town Wentworth only 56 kilometres further on, then it was another 260 kilometres to the next town, Renmark in South Australia, with locks 10, 9, 8, 7 and 6 there to slow us down a little. There appeared to be no towns in this 260 kilometre stretch as the river wound its way up to the far north-west corner of Victoria. It looked a quite remote and desolate part of the country, the back of beyond, well off the beaten track.

From Renmark on we would be in South Australia where the Murray passed through a number of towns before reaching Lake Alexandrina with Goolwa the other side of the lake as the official end of the river. All these towns looked only a couple of days apart so after Renmark we seemed to have places all the way to buy groceries (and a cold beer).

Sturt did this little sojourn we were about to undertake, from roughly where Mildura sits today down to the end of the Murray River, over a few weeks in late February and early March, 1830. Now if it only took Sturt a few weeks to row from Mildura to the lake it meant that a couple of super-duper kayakers like Brian and I should take half that time; surely. But unlike Sturt, Brian and I had no plans to paddle back up the

Murray - we would have a car nearby so we could drive home with our kayaks. Unless we sold them to unsuspecting French tourists telling them to row back up the river if they were after an easy way to reach Khancoban.

A delay

But in late December 2009 we hit a hitch, a brick wall, a real spanner in the paddling works. I received an email from Brian: 'Not sure about next year at the moment. Things are a bit up in the air. My wife has run off with a guy from Tasmania so I am stuck here fixing taps and tidying up the house so I can sell it and get my life back in order.'

Lesson learnt. Have more than an occasional discussion with your friends. I thought I had better be considerate and compassionate with my bosom buddy going through a major emotional upheaval in his life, so I decided to call him and buck him up: as he would need genuine support in his hour of grief.

"She hasn't taken the kayak has she?"

"Nah," was his reply. "Arsehole took the dog though."

I told him to have a few beers, a game of golf, read a book full of lust and sex and in a week he would be back to Tintaldra chasing Miss Brown Legs in the camping ground. What was a delay of a year in our trip anyway? He could sell his house, find a new woman and we could head off from Mildura in twelve months time.

Water everywhere

Brian surfaced a year later, in late 2010, having sold his house and with the news that his ex was still in Tasmania, eating apples and freezing to death (he hoped). He now lived out of a caravan with his worldly possessions spread around three friend's houses, but he had bought an old cottage in

201

Beechworth in north-east Victoria which he was renovating. Art-deco style he told me, which made me regret not visiting the art-deco centre of the Universe, Nyah West, when we passed by the town a couple of years ago. I supposed I was pleased he was alive and well and back in the land of the living, except that I had to go paddling again.

Rain had been dropping itself in bucket loads all across the eastern part of Australia, and in particular the Murray-Darling Basin catchment area from Queensland all the way down to Victoria. We wondered what effect this bucketing rain would have on the Murray River. The Basin has 20 rivers including the Darling, the Murrumbidgee and the Murray and they interconnect in some way or another - so flooded rivers feeding into the Darling and the Murrumbidgee meant a flooded Murray River. Even better, for kayakers looking for added water flows, the rivers feeding into the Murray from Victoria in the south - the Goulburn, the Ovens, and more - were also in flood, pumping copious amounts of water into the Murray.

We both watched the media reports of flooding with interest:

Jan 6. *Weekly Times* newspaper: 'The Murray Darling floods crisis ... the enormous volume of water flowing into the system from the Queensland deluge...the Darling River at Bourke, in northwest NSW, is expected to peak at about 12.3m, with major flooding. Mildura, on the Victorian border with NSW, has been told to expect floods within weeks.'

Jan 13. *Weekly Times*: 'A massive wave of water is making its way down the Darling River to the Menindee Lakes. Ultimately, the Darling floodwaters would reach Wentworth, at its junction with the Murray River.'

Jan 19. *The Australian* newspaper: 'Victoria's flood crisis has worsened, with hundreds more homes being swamped yesterday by a mass of water surging north towards the NSW border, cutting off entire towns and terrifying thousands of residents. There are still ongoing threats, particularly to downstream towns. Residents must be prepared for forthcoming emergencies . . . there is a large expanse of water moving (north towards the Murray River).'

January 21. *Mildura Tourism News*: Visitors to the Riverland are being advised that restricted access continues to apply to some parks and reserves due to recent rain and high water levels in the River Murray. Anyone considering boating or kayaking in a park is encouraged to plan the trip and check with the Murraylands Office to ensure the waters are safe to do so. There are certain areas of national parks closed along the Murray River due to minor flooding. Closures have only been restricted to very low lying flooding in national parks. All towns across the river are experiencing slightly higher and faster rivers, watch for the current and debris.'

My brother-in-law told me that I would be crazy to try to row the flooded Murray River this year. My good wife Suzanne was also concerned about the floods, sending notes to the Victorian State Emergency Service, the Mildura Police and a boat hire shop in Mildura, asking if the river was closed and if not, was it dangerous. The message was that anybody kayaking on the river at the moment would have to be highly experienced. Being 'highly experienced' in our eyes, we ignored all these warnings, planning to meet on the 31st of January at Tailem Bend near the end of the river. We could leave one car there and go back to Mildura together with the kayaks.

Car miles

On January 30th, 2011 I left Coffs Harbour for what I hoped was my last trip down south, to Tailem Bend in South Australia, located on the northern side of Lake Alexandrina. Goolwa the traditional 'end of the Murray' was the other side of the lake, but Tailem Bend was close enough to the end of the river for us. Brian had no intentions of paddling across Lake Alexandrina and if Brian had decided to skip a little paddling I was with him, holus bolus.

On my first night out I was halfway, a fun 12 hour drive - 7am to 7pm - from Coffs Harbour to West Wyalong down in the south-west corner of NSW. It is a big State. I shared a Motel room with my paddle - I could not see anyone stealing my kayak so I left it on the trailer in the street outside the Motel. And if they did, such is life, I would have to turn around and go back home.

The next morning I saw the flooded Murrumbidgee River at Balranald and I cheered loudly to myself at the sight of a strong flow of water – surely this would be helping the water speed in the Murray. I hooted and hollered even more wildly when I crossed the Murray River at Tooleybuc (yes, charming old Tooleybuc from a couple of years ago), as the river level was up to the bank, 10 metres higher than when we battled our way past there in 2009. I also noticed (and admired) flood waters over many paddocks where there were even flowers popping up - nothing beats a drop of water to spruce up a farmer's paddock. It was only 10 hours driving this day before I reached the Tailem Bend Riverside Caravan Park, where my first task was to check out the flow of the river there. I stood on a rise overlooking the Murray and the water seemed to be moving with far more speed than in past years. It all looked promising for the paddle from Mildura.

To pass the time waiting for Brian I worked out the road distance I had travelled so far, on this 'kayaking' trip:

Year - 2006 - Coffs Harbour to Albury, then back to Coffs - 2400 kilometres, plus Albury to Khancoban, then back to Albury - 300 kms

Year - 2007 - Coffs to Albury and return - 2400 kms, plus Albury to Tocumwal and return - 300 kms

Year - 2008 - Coffs to Tocumwal and return - 2400 kms, plus Tocumwal to Swan Hill and return - 560 kms

Year - 2009 - Coffs to Swan Hill and return - 2600 kms, plus Swan Hill to Mildura and return - 440 kms

Year - 2011 - Coffs to Tailem Bend – with a return trip to come, 3400 kms, plus a 400 drive to Mildura as well.

Holy Jesus! I will have driven over 15,000 kilometres in total. I could have driven around Australia, starting at Sydney, through Melbourne, then Adelaide, then Perth, then Darwin, then Brisbane and back to Sydney – that is only 13,500 kilometres. I could have joined the London to Cape Town World Cup Rally - a trip of 14,000 kilometres. No one in their right mind drives 15,000 kilometres to go paddling in a kayak.

Speaking of men not in their right mind, Brian arrived at the Tailem Bend Caravan Park at 10pm. I recommended Brian an egg and bacon roll for breakfast at a nearby truckies roadhouse. I had been there before and felt quite at home in my blue singlet. The check-out lass told us that the tea and coffee was all inside the private truckies room and let us through, which proved my point.

Feathering

It was 400 kilometres by road back to Mildura and almost 900 kilometres by river for our return to Tailem Bend - we agreed it should be a breeze with the water flow from the floods. We chatted away as we drove along, on important topics like football and women's breasts, nothing about each other's health, or personal issues – topics good men friends skirt around. I told Brian that I did not buy any new clothes for this trip and that I had reverted back to my old tent, the one with the rip in the bottom.

Brian informed me that he had misplaced a few items in his marital move, so he shopped in Mildura for a kayak seat back rest and many items of clothing, chatting away to the salesman and any customers within earshot all the while.

As we were about to check out, the store manager came up to us and asked if we were into kayaking, a reasonable assumption having bought a kayak seat, and a wardrobe of kayak clothes. As Brian paid for his gifts to himself I offered to help the guy, who took me down to a row with kayak paddles, soon Brian was trailing along behind.

"Can you explain to me what this little raised section is on these paddles?" the manager asked me. "They all have it. See it is on one side only. Is it a design flaw? Why is it only on one side?"

I held the paddle and showed him that the raised part was where the right hand gripped the paddle, and there was not one on the left side so it could turn.

"See, the left hand feathers as the oar goes forward. The right hand stays fixed on the raised bit."

"Oh, I see. Many thanks for that."

Brian listened to all this, gob-smacked. He could not believe that I, of all people, was asked how to use a kayak paddle, a person who in Brian's eyes couldn't even paddle across a river. I think what ticked him off more than anything was my use of the word 'feathering'.

Happy Birthday

Late in the evening we drove into the Mildura camping ground, remembering that it was now two years ago when we first reached this place, at the end of a slow painful paddle (for me) from Swan Hill. Back then the Murray was barely moving, a low lying, slow moving stream; but not so today as the water was so high it lapped onto the camping ground. The river was full and fearsome, a mass of water sweeping past at a great rate of knots, carrying logs and tree branches along like matchsticks. It looked decidedly choppy out in the middle, choppy enough to put the wind up a novice kayaker (like me).

We woke early, not much after dawn, and Brian was already up and about, walking around whistling and humming to himself. This was most unusual. I even wondered if he was unwell and asked him what was the matter, why all the humming and whistling. He said there was no reason. Then I picked the tune.

"Happy Birthday! You are singing Happy Birthday. It is your birthday, the second of February. Happy Birthday old cock."

"Expecting any birthday calls?" I then asked him. "Like one from the lady over the road, your neighbour, the milkman, the Queen?"

He gave me a sort of triumphant look. "Speaking of neighbours, I do hope I get a call from a sexy German lady who lives next door."

He saw me rolling up my old tent and enquired as to whether I had fixed the rip or not. I said nothing. He looked at me for a few seconds then picked up my tent, found some highly expensive tent patches and glue in his gear, stuck a patch over the rip and gave it back to me. My snake hole was a hole no longer so I was now snake proof; no need for any more sock stuffing. I was impressed. My partner was a man of many talents.

I then put on arm sleeves, a little gift from my good lady Suzanne, to keep the sun off my arms and to keep me cool. They were a light blue colour. Brian watched me closely:

"Have you any idea what you look like in light blue arm sleeves?"

Our know-all map book, River Murray Charts was still in use as it covered the river down to Renmark and it showed us a lock coming up within a kilometre of our start. There was a note in the book: 'Lock 11 operates for downstream traffic on the hour and upstream traffic on the half-hour and can be contacted by UHF radio channel 4'.

We were not heavily into UHF radio equipment so I phoned on my mobile and told the lockmaster that a couple of crazy old coots in kayaks would be coming downstream in an hour. Would it be okay for him to open up the lock and let us through? It was okay for him because the lock was not in operation. The river level was high enough so that so we should be able to simply go over the top of the spillway following the river.

We managed to push the six-days-of-food-stocked kayaks down a grassy slope to the water's edge where we paused to stare again at the river - it appeared just as treacherous as last night. It even seemed to have grown in strength, looking more like a flooded river should look: 'paddle on me at your peril' river, a 'don't be a mug and kayak on me' river. I remembered the warnings – were we pushing our luck?

"Let's go," said Brian, so we went, and with some difficulty we were away from the bank and out into the middle of the river, being bounced along by the fast moving water. We went carefully around the first bend and there was Lock 11. As instructed by the lockmaster we ignored it and over the spillway we went, not that we could see the spillway well underwater.

This is kayaking

We left Lock 11 in hurry, and a big hurry at that. I had dreamt about this sort of kayaking; fast progress with a strong flow of water and seeing the trees simply whizz by. I came close to getting whiplash watching them; well not quite whiplash, but you get the gist.

The current was a clacker, not that we had a knot-gauge to measure its knot strength (miles an hour to you land lubbers), but we certainly seemed to be travelling at six or seven kilometres an hour. We only needed a few strokes now and again to keep in the middle of the strongest flow. I felt like a K1 kayaker (again). Kayaking was a ball. The remarkably wide river spread across the bush land on each side, flooding the countryside. Parks and roads near the river were under water, road signs appeared in the river and the tops of sheds and roofs of riverside buildings were all that could be seen above the water at times.

Our 'river legs' came back and we moved along quite well but after each hour I still needed to stop for a stretch of the legs and a 'hippy-hippy-shake' of the hips. At our lunch break I told Brian to look out for the 860 blue marker (we had started at the 888 mark at Mildura) where there appeared to be a possible short cut at a place named Cowanna Bend. The river looped back on itself and the map book showed a small outlet, so combined with the water overflowing the normal river banks I thought there could be a channel through, potentially saving us a few kilometres. At the 860 sign there *was* a strong outflow of water, so Brian yelled: "Let's go", waved his paddle and shot down the outflow, me tagging along behind. Away from the main river flow we followed a shallow but fast-flowing stretch of water which meandered its way through the bush, hopefully meeting up with the river later on. We went on and on for 20 minutes but then the water flow slowed and we paddled into a huge billabong. There was no outlet flow back onto the river. This I could not understand! The map showed an outlet, as clear as day.

You may like to know that billabong should be written as 'billy-bong" which in aboriginal language means a blind creek. 'Billy' refers to the water and 'bong' means dead – 'billy-bong' is 'water flowing over low level land, and occasionally vanishing amongst the grass'. I have this on good authority from the late Reverend Peter McPherson from a paper he read before the Royal Society of NSW in 1886. His paper was titled: 'Aboriginal Names of Rivers in Australia Philologically Examined', which sounds authoritative enough to me.

The flowing water had certainly vanished so we had only one option - to go back. Fortunately the day was mild and the wind had yet to make a move for the day so we could paddle back to the river, against the current, without a word of complaint from me. Then the current became stronger as we neared the river, fortunately for Brian he had his radio on and couldn't hear me now grumbling away to myself.

Back on the river we then went on for no more than a minute before meeting three guys sitting in the river having a beer, who told us the short cut was 50 metres further on. We had turned a bit early that's all, and within two minutes we had left the Murray once more, zipping down a fast flowing overflow stream to join the Murray again soon after, saving ourselves a good few kilometres.

Brian waved his paddle in the air. "That was a good short cut. I've no doubts that if we had been here two years ago there would have been no flow through, but with the floods there is water everywhere now, not just in the river."

Using a compass on a river

Occasionally we could by-pass more loops in the river by following a steady stream of water across country, through the trees, and ending up back on the main river flow. Using the maps I told Brian where the river would turn and the likelihood of a short cut over a flooded area and he used his compass to head east, west, north or south based on my suggestions. Somehow it worked well.

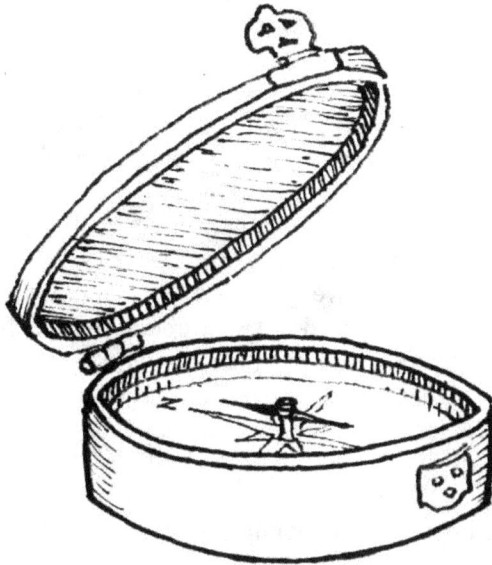

By mid-afternoon we had only twenty or so kilometres to
Wentworth, where the Darling River comes into the Murray.
The thought of a shower at the Wentworth camping site and a
celebratory beer for his birthday at the pub was enough
incentive for Brian to make it there today and with the superb
river flow we closed in on Wentworth just after seven o'clock.
I noticed the camping ground was up the Darling River a short
way, which may have meant some paddling against the current.
However the map book also showed a passage that cut through
to the camping spot, above a large piece of land, named in the
book as a 'sand point' that seemed to split the two rivers. If we
could find that passage it would save us a lot of trouble! Brian
found that gap, and I blessed him. It was now quite late, I was
tired and nine hours paddling was more than enough for me for
the first day; more than enough for me for any day in fact.

We slid through the gap onto the Darling, and there in front of
us beckoned the Wentworth camping ground - a flooded
Wentworth camping ground. A large part of it was well under
water with electricity posts and sign post poles twenty metres

into the swollen river, but there was still a patch of green grass and a few trees out of the water.

A car pulled up alongside us as we walked around. This guy looked about our age, and a wee bit overweight. I went up and looked at him for a few seconds, and said, in as serious voice as I could:

"One of the worst things you can do as you get older is to let yourself become overweight, lazy and indolent. I have a suggestion for you. Why don't you trade your car here for my kayak? A trip from here down the river would be wonderful for you. See the sights. Catch a fish. Camp by the river. I will even drive your car down to the end of the river to meet you and bring you back."

He smiled but he did not take up my offer.

Wentworth is an outback town, not that it looked dilapidated, far from it; it is simply way out back, like in the far south east corner of NSW. To give you an idea just how far outback it is, or was, the *South Australian Advertiser* newspaper in 1860 ran a story explaining that the mailman left Wentworth on his horse every alternate Monday before arriving back at Wentworth the following Saturday. We could have run a faster postal service by kayak.

Wentworth is named after yet another Australian explorer, William Wentworth, not that Willy ever ventured out to this neck of the woods. His forte as an explorer was to find a route up and over the Blue Mountains west of Sydney in 1813. Another claim to fame for Willy was that in 1819 he published the first book written by an Australian (and the worst titled book ever written by an Australian): '*A Statistical, Historical, and Political Description of the Colony of New South Wales and Its Dependent Settlements in Van Diemen's Land, With a Particular Enumeration of the Advantages Which These Colonies Offer for Emigration and Their Superiority in Many*

Respects Over Those Possessed by the United States of America'.

As we walked out of the camping ground we noticed a sign on a large gum tree telling us that Sturt had been here. This was 'Sturt's Tree' and the sign told us that in late January 1830 he had lobbed here and planted his flag to celebrate the discovery of the Darling - Murray junction.

I put my arm around Brian's shoulders. "Pretty cool eh?"

"It is not cool. It's bloody hot. Let's find a pub with air-conditioning."

Back in 1830 Sturt was tickled pink to reach the Darling, '*a new and beautiful stream, coming apparently from the north.*' However, unlike Brian and I saw who saw nothing but a family of wood ducks nearby, Sturt met a large number of aborigines, '*a great body of armed natives, not less than six hundred*' at the gap between the two rivers that Brian and I paddled through. Apparently, the lads were armed to the teeth with spears and boomerangs but they were not as war-like as first thought and soon '*curiosity took place of anger ... and they came swimming over to us like a parcel of seal.*'

Sturt made notes on the difference between the Murray to the Darling:

The strength of their currents must have been nearly equal, since there was as distinct a line between their respective waters, to a considerable distance below the junction, as if a thin board alone separated them. The one half the channel contained the turbid waters of the northern stream, the other still preserved their original transparency.

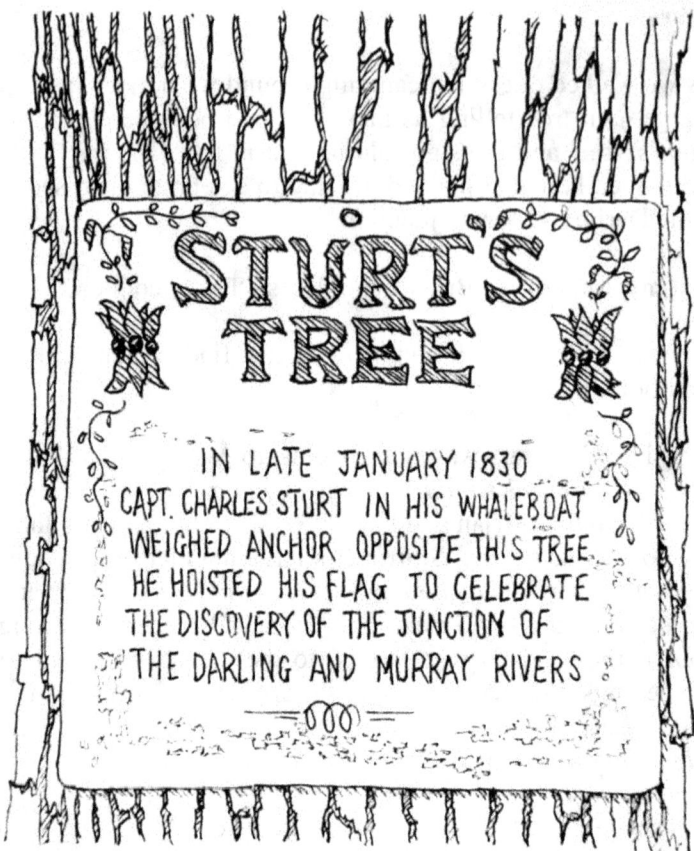

STURT'S TREE

IN LATE JANUARY 1830
CAPT. CHARLES STURT IN HIS WHALEBOAT
WEIGHED ANCHOR OPPOSITE THIS TREE
HE HOISTED HIS FLAG TO CELEBRATE
THE DISCOVERY OF THE JUNCTION OF
THE DARLING AND MURRAY RIVERS

Chapter 19: 'like an inland sea'

[The flooded river continues to push us along. Brian tries to educate me on the heritage of the river. We sit out a two day deluge. A very long day's paddling takes us into Renmark.]

Flying Ants

Mosquitoes and other bugs surfing on the sweat trickling down my chest made for a night of limited sleep but by nine o'clock Brian and I were back on the river, paddling down the Darling a few hundred metres to meet up with the Murray once more. When we reached the junction we saw the same distinctive line between the waters of the Murray and the Darling that Sturt had noticed. The Darling was coffee coloured compared to the black water of the Murray. It was just like adding cream to coffee or mixing up pots of brown and black paint.

Brian did not like the black water of the Murray. He told me it was all due to the flood waters on the leaves and soil and as there had been droughts for a few years there was more debris than normal. Why the Darling was brown he had no idea. He was a fisherman and a bird expert, also a gum tree root system specialist, but he was not a river colour specialist.

We hurried along with the flooded Murray giving us an almighty shove, and we managed to cover sixty kilometres that day. The strong river flow helped and a few short cuts where we cut corners and followed the water through the flooded bush helped too. At times we were not even sure when we were on the river because the water flowed over the banks, overpowering the whole landscape as it swept along ignoring its usual course. It was a huge wall of water and we just allowed ourselves to be carried along with it. Two or three times that day the river did a series of S bends and I would simply tell Brian to go straight ahead if he could, because the river came back on itself. All I had to do was make sure I dodged around the big gum trees lining the river bank.

215

In 1909 a good flood also hit the Murray and the *Sydney Mail* newspaper reported that:

the Murray in flood time is a glorious sight. the river swept down everything that impeded its 'impetuous onrush', cutting off corners and annihilating everything. Fences, haystacks, houses, bullocks, sheep, trees and all kinds of domestic debris were entangled in the 'liquid turmoil'.

The land was like an inland sea, and every red-gum and every box-tree had its 'compliment of snakes, shags and non-descript wild-fowl'.

The 'Sydney Mail' of 1909 had it down to a tee, not that we saw any snakes up a tree, but we did see non-descript wild-fowl and shags.

That night Brian and I camped by a small billabong and the map book showed that we were near the 774 marker – 58 kilometres for the day. In the middle of putting up his clothes line between two trees he suddenly leapt in the air, screaming and hollering. He had walked onto a nest of flying ants and they were all over him. I suggested he should jump in the river, which he did, cursing and cussing as he flew through the air performing what I would have rated as a 7 out of 10 double twisting pike somersault..

"God there is a lot to hate in the Australian bush," he said as he surfaced.

Just as I dozed off that night I heard a gunshot, then a second one, and then it was quiet. 'Duck shooters' I thought to myself. In the morning I asked Brian if he had heard the gunshots, but it turned out they were not gunshots after all, but parts of his bed expanding. It had six separate sections that went down the length of the bed and two of them suddenly blew up and inflated to five times their normal size. His bed now resembled a set of rolling hills and valleys. He managed some sleep by wrapping his legs around the hilly bits and pretending to be cuddling up to a voluptuous roly-poly female. Some dream.

Brian should have brought along a hammock and slung it between two trees. Alfred Wallace, the guy who came up with a theory of natural selection the same time as Darwin, was into hammocks. He goes up the Amazon River in a canoe, collecting birds and beetles and then he wanders around the islands in Indonesia, collecting more birds and even more beetles. Often at night, when he and his native helpers camped, they would sling their hammocks from stakes driven into the ground.

(Brian and I would have needed an axe to make the stakes, as well the hammocks, and possibly a couple of helpers.)

217

Mia-Mia and Muscles

On this part of the Murray we were as far from a town as we would ever be on the trip. I looked at the map book wondering what lay ahead of us in the way of human habitats for the next 200 kilometres and there was little, except for the odd lockmaster. There was an old steam pump marked, a black stump rock mentioned, the site of 'Old Ned's Corner Homestead' listed, and a couple of locks. The day's paddling looked promising.

Brian listened in on his radio and they forecast rain for later on which we hoped would skirt around us. We marvelled at the flood waters each side of the river, and blessed them when they allowed us to skip through short-cutting a bend, saving us another kilometre here and there.

"Look at this," said Brian as we were walking around and stretching our legs at an hourly rest stop. "It is an old native mia-mia."

I looked at bits of bark and twigs leaning up against a stick placed across a couple of trees. It could be - we were miles and miles from any towns or civilisation - we were now in the Wangumma State Forest.

It certainly looked like the real deal, a genuine aboriginal lean-to.

Our observant new-age explorer, Brian Patrick Rock, also found some shells.

"Look here," he called out as he wandered around. "See all these shells? This is a shell midden. You being unlearned when it comes to the way of our indigenous heritage wouldn't realise that these are quite rare away from the coast. A freshwater shell midden is a place where Aboriginal people accumulated shells, after collecting, cooking and eating freshwater shellfish - mussels."

"Speaking of muscles, let's go. My bum muscles are well rested."

Sturt was quite taken by aboriginal huts, writing in his journal on a number of occasions: *several huts were observed by us.'*

He also noted that at times there were *'heaps of muscle-shells scattered about.'*

Mitchell was fascinated by what he and his men saw in aboriginal huts: *'fishing spears, skin cloaks, shields, etc.'* In one hut they found *'some fragments of blue earthenware, nicely attached with gum to threads by which it would appear that the gins wore them in their hair as ornaments.'*

(Now if Mitchell had a mistress, I expect he would have presented her with some fragments of blue earthenware to wear in her hair, to brighten up her day.)

Friendly lock mangers

At four in the afternoon Brian and I drifted up to Lock 8. We could see a house; all the locks were manned twenty-four hours a day by a lockmaster that lived on site. A couple came out of the house and they bought our story that drinking water was all we were after, because the river water was a little too black. They invited us to help ourselves from their rain water tanks, just as a heavy shower of rain started.

This charming couple, Phil and Bec, then offered us the use of a storage room behind Phil's office until the storm passed over - an invitation we accepted, with gratitude and undying love. They asked us what we ate and drank, and no doubt touched by our sorrowful stories they invited us for dinner - barbequed chops and a cold beer - another invitation we accepted, with gratitude and undying love.

I set up my bed in the storage room and Brian set his up next door in Phil's office - the walls looked thick enough to drown out his nasal noises. We showered in a spare shower they had away from their house which was luxury. For Brian an even greater luxury was a sink in the office, with hot and cold running water in which he could wash his undies.

Brian heard on his radio that severe thunderstorms were predicted that could cause flash flooding in parts of Victoria with predictions for three days of severe weather in the wake of cyclones Yasi and Anthony. He also heard a severe weather warning for flash flooding, thunderstorm warnings, damaging winds and large hailstones across the state. We thought we might end up seeing more of Phil and Bec than first planned.

As I watched Brian as he scrubbed away at a persistent stain in his jocks, I thought of our naturalist cum explorer, Alfred Wallace. He was not unlike Brian. He takes an old boat to finally get away from Brazil and heads up towards Bermuda, but it was a clapped out old boat and he had no spare water for washing, so he complains that his shirts were in a state of *'most uncomfortable dirtiness'*. Brian too did not like to be in a state of uncomfortable dirtiness.

It poured down for the rest of the night, not that it worried us. We joined Phil and Bec for a meal and Brian entertained them with a series of Mills and Boon type stories on the various relationships he was now in; one with his German neighbour who Brian said was ten inches taller than him, another with a 'distant' relative, another with a twenty year old who was young enough to be his daughter (or even his grand-daughter), and one with a thirty year old who has seven children. This entertained Bec immensely.

And it poured rain all the next day, heavy bucketing rain too, so we decided to sit it out. Phil did not seem to mind and told us to stay there until it eased - he said no one should be on the river in this weather. Brian dozed on and off, using my flat air bed instead of his heavily contoured one, to catch up on some sleep. His snoring did not seem to worry Phil and Bec - their house was 300 metres away - and with the thundering rain on our tin roof they could not quite hear him. When he was awake he listened to his radio, giving me regular updates.

"There is a warning for Victorians to brace themselves for further rain and flooding today. Torrential downpours and super-cell thunderstorms pounded the state overnight, flooding homes, cutting off major roads and leading to fears of more flooding."

"And, Mildura yesterday recorded a hundred and forty two millimetres, the highest daily rainfall total ever in the town."

The rain started easing that evening so all going well we felt we would be back on the river the next day. I looked at the map book (again) and saw that we had 100 kilometres to go to a lonely spot on the river - called Border Cliffs Homestead - which used to be a Customs House, no doubt the border with South Australia.

There is some logic as to how this isolated spot became the border between Victoria and South Australia. Back in 1846 there was no definite boundary, only a neutral or undefined area where a few shady types made life difficult for the settlers. 'Difficult' in that they picked up a spare sheep when they felt like roast lamb dinner and herded up a few cattle illegally from time to time. The South Australian police chief, a Commissioner Bonney, saw the need to have the eastern boundary of South Australia defined because he was uncertain where his jurisdiction lay – could his men take pot-shots at these bad characters, or not? So the Government surveyors of the day picked a starting point on the south coast, near the mouth of the River Glenelg, and then let a line run due north to the Murray River, marked by scarred trees, surface lines, or piles of stones. Clearly the piles of stones hit the Murray where the Border Cliffs Homestead sits today, which we hoped to pass by in a day or two.

Red hair and the Rufus River

The next day we left Lock 8 at eight in the morning, with 732 kilometres to go to the end of the river. We waved Phil goodbye as he let us through the lock and off we went, scooting down the river again. We had a cool day with a following wind and there were a number of loops on the river we could cut across so it was another day of excellent progress.

"Now old cock," said Brian as we drifted through a flock of flooded red gums, "let me pass on some valuable knowledge about the river. Did you know that river red gums are the only tree which can survive long periods of flooding? Did you know that they grow more in floods than in dry times? Did you know they can take oxygen in through the trunk which is very handy when the roots are flooded and they still need oxygen to respire?"

My response was, "Did you know that we have just bypassed Lock 7 with that last little short cut and there ahead is the 700 sign marker. We've only 700 klicks to go to reach the end of this river."

Bypassing Lock 7 meant we had missed the Rufus River coming into the Murray from the north, but Sturt hadn't, and he named it Rufus after his right hand man, M'Leay, and here is the reason why.

Sturt's party had arrived at the junction of a small river and the Murray, *'where they met aboriginals, a tribe, about 250 in number.'*

Sturt had a rule that they would not distribute any presents *'among the natives'* until they had made them *'all sit, or stand, in a row.'*

This was achieved by Sturt's right hand man, M'Leay, who *'was a famous hand at ordering the ranks'*, and in Sturt's eyes would have made a *'capital drill-sergeant.'*

So, Sturt *'called the little tributary I have noticed, the Rufus, in honour of my friend M'Leay's red head.'*

(Now the relatives of George M'Leay should be rightly ticked off with Sturt that he named this river Rufus, which is Latin for red, rather than M'Leay. Such is life for the M'Leays (the Macleahys these days) - their name does not appear on the map of south west NSW.)

Cross country paddling

Brian and I journeyed on enjoying the river flow, which at one point did a very sharp left turn, just as we faced some magnificent cliffs. This spot was called Devil's Elbow and the map book added: 'this elbow is such a difficult piece of navigation' - not for us kayakers though.

A rare event occurred for in the afternoon - we passed a few canoes and tents on the bank. They were the first fellow kayakers we had seen. One of the campers saw us and asked us where we had come from and where were we headed for, so we hollered back: "Up near the source and Goolwa." They told us they were only paddling from Devil's Elbow down to Renmark. Pansies.

The river was due to turn back on itself after the 660 blue distance marker so I told Brian to take an outlet, which appeared to bypass a loop of the river. Off he shot down the overflow stream, like a mad-man possessed. I couldn't keep up but now and again he stopped and waited for me. At first the water flow was substantial but then it started to slow down as it spread across the bush land, getting shallower and shallower and the current falling away to nothing. Soon we were in shallow still water, only a couple of inches deep, and then we had to push and pull our way through weeds, bushes and little trees.

One particular and prominent shrub we battled through was the home of all things six or eight-legged. We couldn't always paddle around these clumps of bush, so we crashed through them bringing down a shower of spiders and other long legged insects who headed for the inside front of the kayak. Now and again one of them would walk up my leg and peer around to see where it was, muttering in spider-spiel: 'what in the hell am I doing in here?' Now and again one or two would give me a nip and say: 'take me back to my mum and dad'. Now and again I managed to grab one or two and fling them out, cursing: 'piss off you bastard'.

I struggled to keep up with Brian but I faithfully followed him as he forced his way through the reeds and muck until finally, after an hour or so, he called back that he could see the river ahead. At about that time I felt something eight-legged nibbling away at my left buttock, but at least we were back on the river, with current to help us along.

We stopped for the night an hour before dark, just past the 648 blue marker sign. I mentioned to Brian that the guide book showed we were now in South Australia, which pleased us both. I also mentioned that we had had another good day, an almighty good day in that we had covered over 90 kilometres by the blue distance markers, with help from a number of short cuts - we had been paddling for nigh on eleven hours. While knocking in a tent peg Brian managed to strain his back. He started weeping and wailing away, stuck on his hands and knees (well not quite weeping but you get the picture), while all I could think to myself: 'you little beauty, this may slow the bastard's paddling speed'.

We were up early the next day and not for the first time on this trip I made the mistake of mentioning to Brian that we could reach a target – Renmark - if we paddled hard today. Within three minutes he had eaten his Weet-Bix, pulled down his tent, doused the fire, packed his kayak and pushed off from the bank. There he sat, noisily slapping the water with his paddle, waiting for me. He said his back felt alright sitting down with his legs out straight, and not that he wanted to rush to Renmark but he thought we may as well be on the river as sitting here.

It turned out to be a most scenic day. We passed by a series of remarkably impressive cliffs at Queen's Reach, even more majestic cliffs at Bunyip Reach, and to top them all, regal, stately cliffs at a lonely spot called 'Warwilla'. We were both taken in by these 'Warwilla' cliffs as there were columns after columns of rock that looked so close to perfect they could have been hand-made. If Romans had ventured down this way and put up a few columns I imagine they would have looked exactly like the cliffs at 'Warwilla'.

Late in the afternoon we tried another short cut but we had run out of luck with our overflow streams. Half an hour later we were in a stagnant billabong, battling our way through weeds and the dreaded eight-legged creature infested shrub once again. We got caught up on logs, stuck between logs, slowed down by thin weeds, snagged on thick weeds, and bogged in shallow water.

Eventually we had no choice but to go back to the river. Brian got out of his kayak, where the water only came up to his ankles, pulled the nose of it around and back he went. What could I do but follow him - unless I wanted to end up a sliver of peat, for miners to dig out in a million years time. I said nothing, I was absolutely knackered, but eventually we reached the river by which point I was flagging even more. We had been paddling against the outflow current, which became stronger and stronger the closer we got to the river - the river I wish we had never departed from.

We then saw the 572 marker which meant only six kilometres to the Renmark camping ground: we should be able to reach it in an hour. The sun had long gone but in a lingering twilight we soon reached the outskirts of Renmark and with my paddling speed now getting close to first gear, Brian pulled ahead. I told him to get us a tent site.

Chapter 20: 'most pressing invitation'

[We rest for a day. Brian tries to win a heart of a Renmark local. Unbelievably, we become lost in the bush. Back on the river we pass the 500 kilometres to the sea point. There is no joy at Kingston-on-Murray. We have an unwelcome visitor at lunch. We use fresh towels, on a very large boat.]

Kilometres not miles

As I drifted up to the Renmark camping ground in the gloom, I could see Brian 500 metres away, waiting for me way down the other end of the camping area. There were campers laughing, eating, drinking and obviously enjoying life on the river bank. (Was I jealous? Damn right I was.) I decided to see the people at the camp office before going down to Brian, just so we knew where to put our tents.

I stumbled out of the kayak, and staggered my way up to the camp manager's office. I was almost unable to walk, my legs telling me they were not happy to have been stuck in a kayak for twelve hours. It was a cool evening and my shirt and shorts were saturated but I could not find the long sleeved shirt I had tied onto the back of my kayak. The park manager did not comment on my wet kayak shoes, wet pants, wet shirt, blue arm sleeves and sun hat, simply telling one shivering kayaker that we could camp in a non-powered camping area 200 metres off the river, down the back of the camping area. I stumbled back to my kayak, tumbled in, dropping my sunglasses as I did so, and slopped my way down to Brian.

"Hello old son," he said. "I thought I may have lost you. I saw a log floating by with what looked like an old straw hat on top but I think it was a bird's nest. I thought you may have been hit by one of the speed boats."

"Patrick, I'm almost done in. It's past eight o'clock. I've just dropped my sunglasses in the river somewhere. I think I have lost my only long sleeved shirt. We've kayaked for twelve hours. I'm as hungry as a hunter. All we have to do now is lug our gear 200 metres to the non-powered camping spot, then find a pub to eat and drink at, or just drink at."

But it was too late to get up to a pub, as the town centre was a good kilometre away from the camping ground, so we enjoyed a meal in the camp kitchen, drinking cask red wine while eating the best two minute noodles money could buy. I was a happy man. We were at Renmark, two days ahead of schedule and only 566 kilometres from the end. We could even make it.

The next day was our Sabbath, a day of rest, and I needed it. I had a mass of bites on my left buttock, a series of big red spots, which I displayed to the local doctor (my paddling partner) but he was not concerned. I looked around and noticed that a family was camped only 20 metres away, also admiring my well nibbled bum, no doubt the highlight of their day. I expected to hear the sounds of police sirens soon, then to be arrested for indecent exposure, which would have meant Brian with me in the clink, as an accomplice. Thankfully, the family just turned away, Doctor Brian gave me some ointment, and scolded me at the same time for making life difficult for myself – asking me just this once to do him a favour and put it on. Rather than turn my back on the children of the nearby family, I even went into my tent to apply it.

While Brian spent a couple of hours in the camping ground laundry, I looked at what lay ahead for us on the river. Our good bible 'Murray River Charts' stopped at Renmark so we had to change map books to show us the way to Goolwa (the end of the river). I had purchased an old book called 'Murray River Pilot Goolwa to Renmark South Australia'. It looked an excellent book - just like the 'River Murray Charts' – but it was written in 1976 so it could be a little out of date. One note told me that near a town called Mannum, which was coming up, there is a willow tree 'believed to be the largest on the Murray, planted almost a century ago'. I thought of suggesting to Brian that this could be more impressive than seeing the largest gum tree, which I knew for a fact we would never see on this trip.

The new map book had a page of 'A few tips of lore' or 'How to behave in a boat', which told me: 'Do not ever shoot from a boat with a rifle'. I would keep that in mind, if we had a rifle. The book also showed that there were one or two ferries still operating (or there were in 1976 anyway). These ferries were still needed to shunt people across the Murray - possibly they were not as keen on building bridges in South Australia as they were in New South Wales and Victoria. Or more likely some roads were only used by a few local farmers carrying bales of cotton around and they were happy to sit and wait for a ferry to come across on the hour and pick them up. The 'Pilot' book had a note: 'It is a folly to pass in front of a moving ferry. There is no way to tell how far beneath the surface the cables are'. I would keep that in mind should I ever see one of these ferries.

This new book, 'Murray River Pilot', written by Ronald and Margaret Baker and a William Reschke, was laid out just like 'Murray River Charts' with a detailed map of each part of the river, with towns, camping spots, locks and mileages all marked. The other map book had been drawn up by a Maureen Right and included sketches by a Neville Kroemer. They are both well worth a plug as they are a must-have book for any Murray River boatie.

I took our new map book over to the laundry to see how far Brian (the laundry man) had progressed with our clothes. I went and put my arm around him, calling him sweetheart as I did so. An elderly couple were in the laundry too and the lady stared at us in amazement, eyebrows inching up a notch or two. Brian told the couple not to worry.

"He thinks he is being funny. He is a happily married man."

The old couple said nothing.

I went on. "Now Patrick, I have looked at the route we have ahead of us. That last 250 kilometres we did was the only stretch of the river where we had to worry about food. My new map book tells me that we are now only 354 miles from the sea. Notice I mention miles, not kilometres, and this is because the 'Pilot' book was written way back in the dark ages, before the pound became the almighty dollar and the mile became a kilometre and a bit."

I think Brian was listening, as he measured out a large bucket of soap powder to wash our clothes with. I know for sure the old couple were listening.

"The book also shows me that we have towns by the river all the way now. At a point 327 miles to the river's end we pass by Berri, at 304 Loxton, at 238 Waikerie and at 199 Morgan. Up to Morgan the river continues to head west and north-west, although there is the odd wiggle that takes it south, then after Morgan the last 199 miles will all be south, south, and south, all the way to the end."

The old lady butted in with a little trivia: "We've been to Morgan, there's a splendid antique shop there."

"Miles he tells me," said Brian, to the old couple. "Miles went out in the dark ages."

"Don't fret sweetie," I told him. "I have calculated where the blue marker two-kilometre signs will be, assuming they will still be posted from now on."

Of course Sturt produced the first charts of the Murray River, or at least parts of it, from where the Murrumbidgee comes in down to Goolwa.

Sturt was a meticulous chart mapper for a couple of reasons. The first was that he needed to show his taskmasters back in Sydney where the river flowed and all that sort of stuff.

I always had a sheet of paper and the compass before me, and not only marked down the river line, but also the description of country nearest; its most minute changes, its cliffs, its flats, the kind of country back from it, its lagoons, the places at which the tribes assembled, its junctions, tributaries and creeks, together with our several positions, were all regularly noted.

Secondly he guessed he would be coming back up the river at some stage, on his way home to Sydney and on their return journey, because of his earlier note taking, they would have *'no difficulty in ascertaining upon what part of it we were, by a reference to the chart.'*

Heading back up stream would be a tough job but Sturt was keen to make same distances each day, even with *'with the current against us.'* Without the notes and measurements taken on the way down he felt they would have *'often have stopped short of them, weary and exhausted.'*

Boot-scooting at Renmark

By seven o'clock Brian was dressed to kill. He was ready to hit the nightclubs of Renmark, decked out in clean jeans, a flashy shirt and a shiny pair of boots. I thought we were struggling for room in our kayaks but now, low and behold, there he was in an outfit Tex Ritter would be proud of.

"This is my boot-scooting outfit," he explained. "I had to bring it. Tonight may be my first lucky night as an unmarried man and I want to be dressed for it. All we need to do is find a pub with music and a lonely girl at the bar and success is guaranteed."

I thought he was madly in love with his tall German neighbour, (between you and I think he was), - so possibly he was all talk and simply liked wearing a cowboy outfit to the pub. As it turned out there were no nightclubs in Renmark for Brian so he enjoyed his sweetheart's company (me), talking about the art deco décor of the pub. The ladies of Renmark missed out on sampling the good old Brian Rock charm, but the night was not a complete waste as I learnt a lot about art deco which would no doubt be invaluable to me later in life.

Early the next morning Brian the virgin and I packed up camp, lugged our worldly possessions 200 metres across the camping ground to the kayaks, and stuffed everything in. He was concerned that Renmark may be the last opportunity for him to wear his boot-scooting outfit so I told him to put his radio on and listen to some talk back radio. That would relax him.

After a few hours of paddling and a few buttock-kneading hourly stops we were back in the groove. We lunched on a special delicacy of a fresh tomato on unleavened bread which may seem like an insignificant change to a menu but it tasted like whipped cream on a stale bun to a struggling kayaker.

At lunch I passed on some good news to Brian, that the next place of note was a town called Berri which had a licensed store - we had no Guinness or cask wine, as the camping ground in Renmark was located far away from a bottle shop. But not a Guinness could be found at the Berri store would you believe, only West End beer, a South Australian beer which

Brian claimed was the worst ever made. With a choice of West End beer or nothing, we had no choice but to buy it.

From the new map book I saw a possible short cut coming up soon - an outflow was marked before the river turned around a large loop, and it looked like it should meet up with the river again after the river loop. My only concern was a possible billabong away to the south-west, so we had to make sure the outflow went south, not west.

Back on the river we sat and watched the Berri ferry transport people and cars across the river. Noticing the large cables used to pull the ferry across, I kept in mind the Pilot book's 'Tips of Lore' - the folly to pass in front of a moving ferry – if the cables broke they could whiplash a blue plastic kayak into 1000 pieces, and me with it.

We passed the 520 blue marker - our 'Pilot' book may have been in miles but the clerks in the Government Blue Marker Signage Department back in Canberra were up to date – the blue signs were in kilometres. Brian called, "there is the outflow," pointing and off into it he shot. I looked again at the map and didn't like what I saw because the outflow he took headed west where there was a billabong - we had to go south if we were to leave the river. I followed Brian and hollered out to him:

"We must go south Patrick, not west. West will take us away from the river into a billabong."

"Okay. I have my compass out and I see that up ahead there are two flows, one that goes west and the other south, so we will take the southerly one. Follow me."

Off he went following a shallow flow of water and like a lemming I followed. This southerly overflow water stream seemed to meander to the south at first, then to the east, then to the north, then to the west and soon I had no idea which direction we were heading. Brian had the compass so I had faith in him.

Lost on a river

After more than an hour of slogging our way through weed and shallow water the flow slowed right down and then stagnated into a swamp where I recognised some of the spider loving bushes from a few days ago. Brian had stopped as he could not see any outlet so we decided that we had to go back where he thought he saw a better flow, back a little he thought. So we sloshed our kayaks around 180° in the reeds and bushes and then we went back, back what seemed like a little more than 'back a little'.

"Down here I think it is better," said Brian, pointing to a stronger flow of water.

But 'down here' led to another hour of battling through bushes before we ran into yet another swamp, and then we finally ran out of water deep enough for the kayaks.

"Look over there," he said, pointing to some other water flow 100 metres away. "That flow is good; we can pull our kayaks across there and we will be okay."

So we pulled and pushed each of the kayaks across the dirt to the 'flow is good' water; in we hopped and away we went but after what seemed like another hour we hit another swamp and once again we were in drastically shallow water.

"This is not good," said Brian.

I was too tired to talk. 'Let me die here' I thought of crying out but I said nothing. We turned our kayaks around yet again and pulled our way back up stream in search of some good flowing water, but again we hit another dollop of swamp with shallow water and zero water flow. We both got out and walked around and it dawned on us that we were actually lost, lost in the middle of the bush and no idea where the river was. An hour or two ago we thought we could see trees by the river but now every direction looked the same. I did think of bursting into 'Little Boy Lost', a great little Australian classic country song.

"Fame!" I did shout out. "I have always wanted to be famous and now I am. Woo-Hoo! We are the first people ever to be lost on a river. I can hear the questions now: 'Mr. McOrist. Can you tell us how you and your kayaking friend, who you say died of natural causes in the bush and was buried by you somewhere, came to lose your way on a river? My understanding of rivers is that they flow one way and it should be impossible to get lost on a river."

"Then they will ask you who the navigator was. Enough of that drivel, we have to get out of here."

"I have no idea where we are," I said. "If we have been going south most of the time we may not be too far off the river. If we have been heading west then we could be anywhere."

"I think we have been going south, generally," he said. "Let me have a look around."

Surrounded by gum trees the colour of old fence palings I sat on my kayak, the kayak sitting in an inch of water, pondering a night in the bush. It would be pointless trying to ring for help because we did not know where we were, and how could anyone get us out anyway. Brian came back after 20 minutes of wandering around with some good news - there was a gravel road up ahead which went down to a lock. We were on the opposite side to the lockmasters house but there was a place to camp this side, just below the lock. The only problem was there was no water flow to get us there so our only option was to carry our stuff to it.

That is just what I felt like, a tip-top stroll through the bush.

We unpacked our kayaks of all the heavy gear and carried it piece by piece about 300 metres through the bush to the river. It took about ten relay trips as we had water, food, beer and ice, tents, camping gear, and clothes. Last of all we carried each of the empty kayaks to the river.

We then sat down and looked at each other, neither of us saying a word for a while, but thinking how first rate it was to be back by the river. We had been hacking away in the bush for about five hours. We opened up a West End beer and Brian endorsed my proposition that it was the best beer man ever made.

500 to go

The next morning we felt okay, nearly human. We were in one voice that we would avoid swamps, take no more short cuts, never detour through billabongs, and stick to the river, the one and only wide Murray River with its never ending current.

The plan for the day looked straightforward, a town called Loxton was coming up in about twenty-five kilometres and we would be going south most of the way there. Then the river headed back north-west, and included in that section was what the Murray River Pilot book called the 'Seven Mile Reach', claimed to be the longest straight stretch on the Murray, a whole seven miles long. We prayed for a south easterly tail breeze when we got there.

We enjoyed the morning, cruising along without a lot of paddling effort and generally in a southern direction although the river looped around close to 360° at times. Brian had a ball searching for eagle's nests in the trees and straining his beady eyes for anything on the cliff faces we passed. He listened to his radio as he floated along, hearing that there was music on Friday night at a club in the town of Waikerie. He wondered when we would be getting there, so at the next rest break I checked the Pilot book and I worked out we would be there tomorrow night: Friday night."

"Excellent," he replied. "I can get to wear my boot-scooting outfit again. Music at the Waikerie club is just what I need. "

We kept knocking over the kilometres, at a rate of about six an hour, and in the afternoon we passed the 500 kilometres to the end of the river sign - that was a significant milestone for us. Only 500 kilometres to go!

By late afternoon, at the 464 marker, the river turned sharply to the north-west and we were at the start of 'Seven Mile Reach'. As we went around the bend we stopped and looked ahead at the river heading away from us in a straight line, as far as we could see. Usually we could see a row of trees ahead indicating where the river next took a turn, but not so here – the river hit the horizon, way, way ahead.

We started to look for a camping spot, thinking they may be hard to find on a straight stretch of water, and they were. Camp sites were usually at a point when the river curved, so that a sand bank, or a mud-bar, or shallow water would appear, on the inside bend of the curve. We ground our way along, into a head wind, inching our way up this seven mile stretch. The land each side of the river was flat and tree-less. There were none of our grand old gum trees here; just scraggly bushes and scrubby shrubs on dirt banks. In the fading light we chose a muddy bank by a small inlet to stop at for the night - it was the best we could find as the sun had well-nigh dropped out of sight.

I then had to beak the bad news to Brian that although I said we would get to Waikerie tomorrow, Friday night, I had made a slight misread on the distances and we would get to Waikerie on Saturday, not tomorrow. He was not a happy camper. He had an aching foot courtesy of walking through a patch of bindi-eyes in bare feet, he was drinking disgustingly warm red wine, he knew he was soon to be attacked by an armada of mosquitoes, and I had just told him his promised boot-scooting Friday night at Waikerie was no longer on.

I tried to brighten up his day as we set off the next morning by telling him it was only 462 kilometres to the sea. He was still not as chirpy as normal, possibly worried that his foot may be too sore for boot-scooting on Saturday night. We pulled our way up the seven mile stretch, straight into a head wind. After that the map showed that the river turned and ducked and weaved (as rivers do), but it still headed in a general north-west direction. There was a town called Moorook to look forward to, and another, Kingston-On-Murray. Brian was happy to stop at Moorook but not Kingston-On-Murray for some unexplained reason.

Near the 446 marker there looked like a possible short cut coming up which we decided to take only if we were a hundred percent certain it would take us back to the river. And as luck would have it, there was strong outflow to the north, so down it we went. After 30 minutes, however, the outflow became wider, slower and shallower, so we stopped and looked at each other. We were in a swamp.

"There are various events in one's life that are significant," I said. "So significant that one learns from them. Such a significant event is being lost for hours in a swamp a couple of days ago. Such mistakes should be so imprinted in the mind that one never repeats them."

Brian nodded and we turned around and struggled back up this outflow, but finally we were back on the Murray, thinking how much we loved the river compared to billabongs and swamps. Again, we pledged to stay on the river to the end.

Later that morning we reached Kingston-On-Murray; a pleasant looking town with a grassy park area and trees for shade by the river. I needed to stop for a stretch and to adjust my seat padding, but Brian did not come into the shore with me; he waited out in the middle of the river - which was most unusual. At every other rest stop the both of us had gone to the bank, hopped out and walked around together - but not this one. After we set off paddling together again I asked him why he didn't take a walk there. We had been paddling for an hour since the last break and it was a fine looking town, Kingston-On-Murray.

"Prick of a town," he said. "That is the town where my ex-wife and her boyfriend went off for a weekend when she decided he was a better bet than me."

How sad I thought. No wonder the boy was in a quiet mood that morning. What could I say? I could say nothing, so I said nothing.

After a few more bends we approached Lock 3 and we could see large yellow balls all across the spillway - the spillway was closed, so we had to go through the lock. My good Pilot book told me that 'to signal required passage through a lock, sound three long blasts from a horn or siren at least half a mile from the jetty'.

We had a lot of things (like noodles and duct tape) but no ship's horn. We did, however, find the lockmaster and the kind man opened up the lock, let us in, closed the back doors, dropped the water to the level of that below the spillway, and opened up the front doors for us to paddle out. This always seemed like a lot of work to do for a couple of kayakers, but apparently they have to do it for all water craft because the river was here before the locks, so they have to allow passage for anyone.

Snake Log

At one o'clock we pulled into the shore to stop for lunch, and I laid out our standard meal on a big log.

"Sardines, a tomato, cheese, unleavened bread and a warm fruit juice," I said. "A lunch fit for a King, and laid out beautifully on this large log, which is the closest thing to a varnished table top I could whip up for you and if I may add, is the closest thing to a snake log I have ever seen."

Brian made himself a sandwich and walked around to the end of the log.

241

"Not only is this the closest thing to a snake log you have ever seen but it also happens to be an actual snake log. Come and look."

"Jesus!" I cried out, looking in at a large black snake staring back at me. "It is a snake log!"

Sturt made mention in his notes that he scared the living daylights out of a few aborigines when he took a pot-shot at a snake swimming across the river. At first Sturt's men attempted to kill it with their boat-hook, but the snake slipped away and then appeared again at some distance. One of Sturt's men put *'a bullet through his head'* which *'soon stopped him in his tracks.'* Apparently the aborigines were not impressed by the loud gunshots, but Sturt's man *'held up the snake to show them reason for the shooting.'*

Captain Moonlight

We did not attempt to kill our snake with a boat-hook, not that we even had a boat-hook, but it was simply a thirty second lunch break before we were back in the kayaks. I called Brian over, both of us laughing nervously that for some reason we would rather be in our kayaks looking at the map than sitting by that log. We discussed the pledge we made that morning, the pledge that could not be broken, because in about two kilometres there was a creek that ran off to the left and if it was navigable it would cut off Overland Corner, saving us a kilometre or two.

This would mean missing out on having a beer at the Overland Corner Hotel, known as Captain Moonlight's watering hole, a pub built in 1859 as a place for overland drovers to wet their whistle. Stories go that in the 1870s a Captain Moonlight used this hotel. He was a man who dabbled into both lay preaching and bank robbing, which finally resulted in a restful time in prison, before he had a go at bush-ranging. Moonlight used to drink whilst still on horseback with the front and back doors of the hotel open in case a couple of coppers walked in, also hoping to down refreshing ales. If we had called in we could have had a couple of beers while sitting in our kayaks and paddles at the ready - in honour of Moonlight.

But with all this water in the river we thought this creek may be flowing and Brian was quite firm on the principle that pledges are made to be broken, (like marriage vows), so we

243

gave it a go and the creek turned out to be flowing powerfully. Before long we were back on the river, saving a good kilometre or more.

We started passing houses and boat ramps on the left hand side of the river, and then a brace of cliffs joined us along the right hand side. These cliffs were even more spectacular than others we had passed, rising straight up out of the water and staying perpendicular, a hundred metres high. We stopped paddling and gazed in admiration letting the current take us by, slowly and quietly. They were impressive, and we also saw a set of large caves at their base. Suddenly the wind picked up and rain clouds closed in so we decided to camp, not in the caves but opposite them, on a made-in-heaven camping spot with soft grass and sandy soil. We quickly put up Brian's tent-fly across some trees just before the rain started, a drizzle at first then down it came, in bucket-loads.

From three o'clock until six o'clock we sat huddled under the fly, keeping dry, enjoying West End beer, eating peanuts and talking the sort of senseless drivel you would expect from two guys drinking warm beer under a tent-fly in the rain. I noticed we had stopped opposite Cave Cliffs, which made us 413 kilometres to the end of the river. We were at a place called Wigley Flat, not that that meant much to Brian and I, or to you probably. Our next place of interest was the scene of Brian's hoped for night out on the town – Waikerie - only 34 kilometres away. We could easily manage that the next day. There was a camping ground mentioned at Waikerie, but the book only read, 'Showers at Caravan Park', not 'Showers at Caravan Park by the river', which worried us a little.

The rain finally stopped but we decided against moving on, so we camped, in as gem of a spot as we could have wished for with bindi-eye free grass and a neat swimming hole. It was all totally private, no people anywhere for miles, and what a view we had with those cliffs opposite - they were corkers! We lit a fire, Brian washed his clothes and then spent 30 minutes erecting a quite magnificent clothes drying apparatus made up of a logs, branches and twigs, all done in a lattice style frame. The man liked dry clean clothes and just maybe he drove his ex-wife nuts with his washing. I made a mental note to ask her one day.

By the morning the rain had cleared. We had travelled no more than fifty metres when we saw a huge expanse of lawn, right next to where we had spent the night, then a set of large gates, a flashy boat ramp and a road up to a house.

"Well, bugger me," Brian said. "I didn't realise we were so close to a house. I thought we were miles from anyone. They could have been watching me scrub my undies in the river."

Women, or the lack of them

We made Waikerie by early afternoon and we beached next to the 'Murray River Queen', a gigantic paddle boat with three or four decks of cabins. As we feared the camping ground was half a kilometre away from the river - too far to carry our gear - so we accepted the caravan park lady's offer of a room ($50) on the 'Murray River Queen'. The boat was closed to the public because the river was due to peak with the floods in the next day or two and the gangway would be under water. She supposed that a couple of kayakers like us should be able to handle a bit of water on a gangway. She was right, and we had the boat to ourselves, except for a security manager who told us all about the 'Queen'. It was the largest side-wheeler paddleboat on the river, holds 60 people, used to be a river cruise boat and then moored at Goolwa as a backpackers' lodge before it came to Waikerie. It was all ours on this day.

We showered in our cabin en-suites, enjoying the shampoo and fresh clean towels provided before adjourning to the top deck, the poop-deck we presumed. My partner was hot-to-trot, ready to hit the dance floors of Waikerie. I hoped he could duplicate Wallace's efforts when he was up the Amazon somewhere and he arrived at an Indian village where a dance was taking place. Wallace wrote:

245

Almost all of them were naked and painted and wearing various feathers and other ornaments. The wild and strange appearance of these handsome, naked, painted Indians, with their curious ornaments and weapons, the stamp and song and rattle which accompanies the dance, the hum of conversation in a strange language.

Later that evening we did case the Waikerie Club but to Brian's disappointment there was no music on Saturday night, and not a naked women to be seen, so I am unable to fill these pages with reams of wild sex. Likewise, if you read the journals of Sturt and Mitchell from the 1800s you won't find much hot action; but they did mention the fairer sex a few times.

Mitchell at one time was quite taken with the daughters of one aboriginal woman. To Mitchell she was '*the handsomest female I had ever seen amongst the natives.*' The girl had light coloured skin, '*so far from black that the red colour was very apparent in her cheeks.*'

Mitchell compared her to a '*fine statue of Eve at the fountain; and apparently equally unconscious that she was naked.*'

The tribal elder, who had obviously seen Mitchell's casual glance or two at the girl, '*begged me to accept her in exchange for a tomahawk!*'

Sturt, like Mitchell, displayed the utmost sensitivity towards aboriginal women. He tells us he '*was particularly careful not to do anything that would alarm them, or to permit any liberty to be taken with their women.*' The aborigines could not fathom why Sturt and his men were not interested in their women, or travelled without female companions. They asked '*questions, by signs and expressions, as to whether we had any women, and where they were.*'

On another occasion Sturt was being followed by a large group of aborigines, '*many of them had their spears, and their*

246

attention was evidently directed to us.' The aborigines used their women to try and entice Sturt and his men to cross the river – believing they could not resist the ladies (for a bit of slap and tickle).

Shortly after this, eight of the women, whom we had not before noticed, came down to the water side, and gave us the most pressing invitation to land. Indeed they played their part uncommonly well, and tried for some time to allure us by the most unequivocal manifestations of love.

But Sturt's men saw through the ruse as they *'observed the spears of the men among the reeds'.*

Chapter 21: 'a line of cliffs'

[The river turns south at Morgan. We marvel at the stunning cliffs near Nildottie. Gale force head winds slow us down. We enjoy sleeping in a bed at Murray Bridge. Brian's final thoughts are on the big Gum tree.]

We could 'almost' smell the sea

By eight o'clock the next day we were back on the river with our target for the day Morgan, a town about 60 kilometres away. Morgan was significant to us, not only because we would then be only 300 or so kilometres from the sea, but, going by the Pilot book, and we had nothing much else to go by, the river suddenly turned south at Morgan and stayed south all the way to the end. This meant we would then be on the final stretch, our 'home straight' to the sea. The end was in sight.

Brian asked if there were any short cuts, but the river now seemed to follow the cliffs so there would not be any overflow water. However, the river did seem to do a complete loop back on itself at one stage near a set of cliffs - at a place the book calls 'Markaranka Flat'. If there was a good flow along the cliff face (and I mean a very good flow), we thought we may be able to cut off that loop.

In spite of our original pledge to never take another short cut (which we had only broken once) we did take that short cut route and it did save a few kilometres. It was a worth-while detour as we drifted along in the shade of trees, close to a cliff face, with a reasonable flow of water. For some reason bunches of ducks dotted the route, which made it quite charming. Technically ducks come in 'rafts' not bunches, and they are known as a 'team' when they are in flight. They are also known as a 'paddling' when on the water. Me, I like the word bunch; it has a sort of duck ring to it.

248

Morgan was originally known as North West Bend, the Great Bend or the Great Elbow, and it became a point for overlanders, on their way to Adelaide with stock, to leave the Murray and make for Adelaide. To make life a little easier for the overlander lads, a steam railway line was opened for traffic in 1878. A wharf was also built at this time- 62 metres long and nine metres above the summer river level, and the place became a focal point for river traffic; but like Echuca upstream, the railways ultimately spelt doom for the river trade.

Sir William Morgan, premier of South Australia at the time, wanted his name to remain etched on all State maps so the town name was then changed to Morgan. In the good-old days, Morgan was the second biggest port in South Australia, shooting out six trains a day down to Port Adelaide, but today, it is a quiet dot on the map, with 850 or so country folk living there, looking after the restored wharf precinct and the town's museums. Brian and I, keen avoiders of museums, were nevertheless suitably impressed by a huge 100 year-old railway turntable, built to facilitate the turning around of railway engines in the rail yards.

We could see the pubs only a short walk from the camping ground but there was not a lot else to interest us in Morgan, except the antique shop which we found while strolling the lonely streets after dinner. Brian stood there wide eyed for half an hour, staring at piles of art-deco paraphernalia, like a schoolboy staring at sticky buns in a cake shop. He said he was tempted to come back here after we finished the river. Fortunately it was ten o'clock and he could do no more than stare, and drool at sets of chrome folding trays, ceramic book ends and marble photo frames. I led him away by the ear lobe, reassuring him that it would all be there when he drove back in a few weeks time because I doubted many people would share his interest in chrome folding trays, ceramic book ends and marble photo frames. But I may be wrong.

With the Murray River Pilot book in short supply back in 1830, Sturt bumbled along here not sure where the river would go to next. However an aboriginal tribe was following their boat and *'there was an old man, who took an uncommon fancy'* to one of Sturt's men.

The old man *'got into the boat and as far as we could understand from his signs,'* they were close to a change in the river. The old man *'pointed due south, as if to indicate that such would be our future course'*, and then went on to describe *'the roaring of the sea, and the height of the waves.'* It was clear to Sturt that this old man had been to the coast.

The old man left them, and rejoined them later, after the river had no doubt looped back a little, and *'his joy at being received into the boat was unbounded.'*

When the old man finally left Sturt's party, Sturt wrote that *'we were really sorry to part with him.'*

(How sweet is that story?)

Lock Number 1 – the last lock

We left Morgan at eight the next morning at the start of our final leg and it felt like the start of the run home, with only 318 kilometres to the end of the river, all in a southerly direction. We prayed for a northerly breeze, a tail-wind. We were quite sure that there were no more possible short cuts as the map book showed no loops or serious bends of any sort.

We headed off aiming for Blanche Town, 45 kilometres away, with the river now quite broad and the current slow. Massive, majestic cliffs joined us on the left bank, towering over us and staying with us for a few kilometres, like an unbroken wall. We saw cockatoos, eagles, and other birds. The cockatoo calling reminded me of Howlong, when we passed by there, in my past kayaking life. By five o'clock we were through Lock

250

1, the last lock, which cheered us up, and at the Blanche Town caravan park soon after.

The next morning we had a southerly into our faces but it was only a gentle breeze so life was rosy. Now for those who yearn for the romantic era of paddle steamers and wish to experience what life would have been like on the river 100 years ago, head for this part of the Murray. Large paddle-boat steamers passed us by, heading upstream with their steam engines droning away, the passengers waving glasses of booze at us. They may have been tipsy, but they all seemed very happy to see us as we paddled by. Being so close to the end, Brian and I were also very happy; happy with anyone and everyone in fact, even slightly sloshed people on a paddle-boat.

Wild weather

Mid-afternoon the wind increased and the weather didn't look promising. We could see a huge rain cloud moving our way, as black as midnight, so we decided to pull into the shore and sit it out. Our squally wind suddenly became very fierce, and then rain started bucketing down so we rushed to get one tent up quickly, but it was already too late. The rain became a torrent, a deluge of a waterfall, and the howling wind became even more ferocious. The two of us struggled to erect the tent as it flapped and billowed about in what was now a hurricane of a storm. In my rush I put the clips on the wrong pole and the fly on back to front so we couldn't get in straight away. All the time we were being deluged by the rain, sheets of water pummelling us and pouring into the tent, but finally we had the tent up and secure, and then we were inside. Saturated we sat together in an inch of water while the wind howled and scowled and the tent shook and shuddered. The frame bowed inwards pushing against our faces so we lay down in the water, with sprays hitting us when the wind whacked against the tent.

"I cannot work out why most women don't like camping," I said.

It continued this way for two hours and we did not say a lot as it was on the verge of being farcical. Brian lay there with a towel over his face and I had one arm stretched up to keep the tent side from hitting my face, until I heard him snoring. Holy Jesus, how could anyone sleep in this?

When the wind eased and the rain dropped to a steady pitter-patter we went outside. The rain had filled up my seating area of the kayak and it had seeped into the rear compartment so my sleeping bag and sleeping mat were water logged. In light drizzling rain we stripped off and put on our transparent plastic honchos over our underpants; a charming sight, as you can imagine.

The next morning was cool but we had a clear sky and were perky - not much more than 200 kilometres from the end of the river, with only 160 kilometres to my car. 'How good is that?' I thought.

We were scheduled to pass a town called Nildottie, which means 'smoke signal hill' from the aboriginal word ngurltartang. I could see from our map book that cliffs were marked at Nildottie, then the river seemed to follow a cliff face for most of the day, down to a place called Walker's Flat, then Bowhill, then Younghusband. I thought Walker's Flat may do us for the day as that was fifty-five kilometres from where we were, but Brian was chomping at the bit.

"Let's see how we go. I now have the sniff of the end in my nostrils, so keep up with me."

Cliffs and more cliffs

We passed by cliffs that morning that left all the others on the
Murray for dead. They were monumental, out of this world; a
shimmering gold colour in the sunlight and changing to a
ginger, copper or rust colour in the shade. The cliffs were close

to vertical, a hundred metres high and we slowly paddled alongside, only a metre or two away. At times we drifted along in the shade hugging the left southern bank and this made the paddling even more pleasant, especially when the river took a bend and narrowed, making the current stronger than ever.

(Here is a travel tip: Go to Nildottie if you want to see the crowning point on the Murray - the Nildottie cliffs.)

Like us Sturt was impressed by the cliffs along this part of the Murray. First of all he tells us of one series of castle-like cliffs - these were the regal, stately cliffs at 'Warwilla' that Brian and I had passed a few days ago.

The left bank of the Murray was extremely lofty, and occasionally rose to 100 feet perpendicularly from the water. It is really difficult to describe the appearance of the banks at this place; so singular were they in character, and so varied in form.

Here they had the most beautiful columnar regularity, with capitals somewhat resembling the Corinthian order in configuration; there they showed like falls of muddy water that had suddenly been petrified; and in another place they resembled the time-worn battlements of a feudal castle.

But the cliffs that most impressed Sturt were those that Brian and I were passing by. He too was taken by their height, their colour, and on his day he could see aborigines, but not us, on our day. As he sat up the front of his boat, quill in hand, Sturt wrote:

... a line of cliffs, of from two to three hundred feet in height, flanked the river, first on one side and then on the other, varying in length from a quarter of a mile to a mile.

They rose perpendicularly from the water, and were of a bright yellow colour, rendered still more vivid occasionally by the sun shining full upon them. The cliffs under which we passed towered above us, like maritime cliffs, and the water dashed against their base like the waves of the sea. They became brighter and brighter in colour, looking like dead gold in the sun's rays; and formed an unbroken wall of a mile or two in length.

The natives on their summits showed as small as crows; and the cockatoos, the eagles, and other birds, were as specks above us; the former made the valley reverberate with their harsh and discordant notes.

The guru makes a mistake

Brian and I travelled so well that we only stopped for a break once before lunch, me with no aches and pains for a change. At three o'clock we ate a late lunch at the shop at Bowhill, and the next town in our sights was Younghusband less than 20 kilometres on, three hours away.

I quickly pushed off from the bank, trying to get a few minutes start on Brian, as I often did. I would keep paddling but after ten minutes I would usually hear him coming up behind me by the sound of his paddle splashing. But this time I heard no paddling splashes, so I kept on going. After half an hour I was concerned, a little, not a lot, but I thought I had better turn sideways and see where he was. I looked back and there he was 500 metres behind, paddling away like fury. He must have seen a fish, I thought, so I went back to my paddling until he eventually caught up.

As unbelievable as it sounds, he went the wrong way. I wondered how one could go the wrong way since the river goes downstream in one direction, but he explained that where we had stopped there was not a lot of current and after a few minutes he could not see me ahead so he realised he was going upstream, not down. He turned around and saw me, half a kilometre ahead.

My day was made! The great kayaking guru had finally cocked something up, by going the wrong way. I laughed so much I all but tipped my kayak. However I promised never to tell anyone that he went the wrong way. My lips were sealed. No one would ever know.

By the time we pulled up outside the Younghusband store and camping ground the sun had left us and my body felt almighty tired and cold after an 11 hour paddling day. Everything was closed and we were alone, save a couple of pelicans who lingered around hoping for us to throw them a few of our fish scraps. They did not linger long as we did not have any fish scraps for ourselves, let alone for a couple of pelicans.

That evening, in the gloom, I could feel the end of the river. We had less than a hundred kilometres to go. Today was a big day as we had covered seventy kilometres, and actual kilometres as we had no short cuts so it was no wonder I was a little buggered. I had become cold by the end of the day, being saturated from the paddle drips and chilled by the wind especially after the sun left us. Brian promised to have a look at my paddling technique in the morning to fathom out why I managed to collect so much water off my paddle.

We thought we may get to Murray Bridge the next day as we were now only 56 kilometres away, and from Murray Bridge it was only 20 to Tailem Bend, where I hoped my car was. I was reasonably certain that my almost illegal, certainly unsafe and very un-roadworthy trailer would not have been stolen.

A 13 hour day on the river

Brian and I were up early. It was cloudy, and windy. The river has risen during the night, and the corner of my tent was under water, but nothing was too wet inside, except my kayaking shirt which was wet from yesterday anyway. Brian saw my wet shirt and that reminded him to look at my paddling style. He reckoned there must be a flaw – why did I get so wet and he stayed as dry as a bone.

He noticed my paddle blade was quite different to his. Mine was like a scoop, bucket shaped, but his was simply curved a little on each side. I picked up his paddle to look at it more closely and realised a bigger difference - his paddle was as light as a feather! He offered me the use of his paddle but I said thanks but no thanks. I had battled on so far with a heavy paddle, wet clothes and being frozen most of the time, so I had to finish the same way.

"Lord give me strength," he exclaimed. "The martyr! That's what you are a martyr. And that's what we are 'the scruffy martyr and the resplendent gentleman'. Good name for your book if you ever write one."

We were on the river early, to be greeted by a strong southerly wind, blowing straight into our faces. We hoped it would soon die down – but die down nothing. The wind not only started out with vigour it picked up speed and soon turned into a blast of brute force. The river was wide and the current was slow so it was a day of head down, bum up, and pull hard. We did not look at the scenery; Brian did not comment on any birds and he even refused to cross the river to read a distance marker. We stuck to the edge of the river with the most shelter from the wind because in the middle it was always rough, with waves capped by white caps.

It was eleven o'clock before we had our first rest, at Mannum. The squally head wind had continued and at times we hardly seemed to be making any headway. If we stopped paddling we went backwards against the current. There were no frequent stops on the bank because willow trees and reeds now lined the river. I may add here that the last thing in the world we felt like doing was to look for the: 'willow believed to be the largest on the Murray, planted almost a century ago'. I may also add here that the Pilot book made reference to this part of the river as a notorious stretch of water, exposed to all winds, and if they were from the south-west or west the river could have violent choppy water and white caps: 'not to be taken cheaply by small boatmen' said the book - we did not take it cheaply, trust me.

Finally, in the early afternoon, after six hours, the river turned to the east and we had an hour with a side wind, which meant we could paddle along the edge using the trees and reeds as a wind break. We even tried singing some songs to take our mind off the agony of it all.

"This time Patrick I have picked sing-along songs. These are songs that any person can sing to without needing a musical accompaniment."

And away the pair of us went, paddling as hard as we could, singing on the tops of our voices:

> *"This land is your land,*
> *This land is my land."*

"I like that song," he said when we had finished. "And we must have covered at least a hundred metres while singing it."

And away we went again:

> *"Hang down your head, Tom Dooley*
> *Hang down your head and cry."*

258

"Patrick, I cannot sing anymore," I said. "I am not sure I can paddle any more either. My arms are about to fall off."

"You need a five minute rest McOrist, that's all. We will pull over when we see a spot."

But we could not find a place to pull into and rest. Then the river swung south once more and we were back into a strong headwind and I did not like the look of what lay ahead. By the map book the river went due south for ten kilometres, straight into this roaring snorting gale.

Brian asked me on which side of the river we should travel. I was not sure why he asked me - he was usually a far better judge of all river matters, but I guessed the left side. By the map book the river seemed to swing slowly to the right later on so I thought that should give us some protection from the wind. The man followed my advice, the bloody fool. I had picked the wrong side of the river - as the river slowly turned it only brought us into the direct face of the wind.

My God, it was then hard work. I would pick a bush or a tree about 30 metres ahead on the bank and make that a short term goal. 'In, push back, other side, in, push back, other side, in push back.' It was nonstop, relentless, but there was no choice, we had to keep paddling otherwise the wind would have taken us back to Albury, well not quite Albury but at least back into the large willows behind us. Willows and reeds still ran their dominating show on the river bank - the good old days of a rest on the hour were a distant memory.

We soon realised that my judgment call of which side of the river to travel was wrong. Brian yelled to me that we had to go over to the other side, and off he went, battling his way across the river, about 500 metres wide. Large waves rolled down the river with the wind, and plenty of whitecaps too but I followed him, being careful to not push the oar in hard when there was a dip in the water by the kayak because of the swell, and riding carefully across the whitecaps. It took some time, but finally I joined him on the other side, where there was a little bit of shelter from the wind, but not a lot.

We had no other option then but to push on, and push on we did, for another four hours before the river finally turned back to the west and some cliffs gave us some shelter. We took a few deep breaths, offered each other little in the way of conversation before paddling on, looking for a rest spot. They were still hard to find, until finally there ahead of us we saw a grassy area, just before a large pumping station. We lay there on beautiful, soft, warm grass and rested; eating the last of our supplies, a few chocolate and nuts. I suggested we camp there but Brian said we should push on, as Murray Bridge was now 'only' twelve kilometres away. We had about three hours of daylight left and we could be there by dark, if I could keep going.

Back in 1830 Sturt met strong winds along this section of the river, '*a succession of gales from the S.W., against which we, on several occasions, found it useless to contend.*'

He described the waves as being '*heavy and short*' and the boat, driving into them, '*sent the spray over us and soon wet us through.*'

He felt that it would be '*difficult for the reader to imagine the heavy swell that rolled up the river, which had increased in breadth to the third of a mile.*'

He, or should I say his men, '*found it very distressing to pull against the heavy breezes that swept up the valley.*'

In a lovely turn of phrase he says the wind '*bent the reeds so as almost to make them kiss the stream.*' They eventually found progress impossible; the wind gusts '*prevented us from making an inch of way.*' His '*men were quite exhausted*', so they pulled in to bank and pitched their tents for the night.

The last paddle to Murray Bridge

After another three hours of dog-tired paddling I had another look at the map book. Joy! We were now in the last section of the river before Murray Bridge. I saw that within a kilometre the river would turn left and around the corner we should see a bridge, and that would be Murray Bridge.

Down we went to the corner and then around it, Brian leading the way as you would have expected.

"See the bridge?" I yelled.

"Not yet."

Then five minutes later, "see the bridge?"

"Not yet."

Then five minutes later, "See the bridge?"

"Yes."

"You little bloody beauty!" I screamed out.

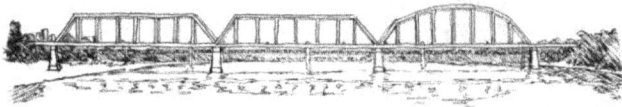

Not that Brian or I gave a hoot, but this bridge just happens to be the first bridge built across the Murray River. Its construction in 1879 was big deal at the time - the first permanent crossing over the Murray to link the South Australia colony with eastern Australia. Before then, ferry and punt

261

crossings were the only way people could head east, or west for that matter.

Last meal – noodles for Brian

Finally, we were at the township of Murray Bridge. The sun had long nose-dived over the horizon leaving us in the gloom to find a camping ground. I was tired, hungry, soaking wet and freezing cold but apart from that, okay. We asked a couple on the wharf where the camping ground was and they told us it was down the river a bit, on an island but it was a fair way out of town. Brian was not impressed. He (and I) needed a hot shower; we needed a cold beer, a large piece of steak and a soft warm bed. We did not need to go 'down the river a bit' to a camping ground so Brian suggested we pull into the shore, leave the kayaks in a safe place and find a pub to stay at for the night.

He had no argument from me. Finding a safe place for the kayaks was difficult but we left them next to the Murray Bridge Rowing Club. (I thought: with luck someone might nick them in the night). We pulled out our clothes and toiletries and headed up to the town, me carrying one small clothes bag and my paddle, Brian carrying five large clothes bags, and his paddle.

Clutching our worldly possessions we staggered into a hotel. "$55 a night for a double room or $44 each for a single room," said the lady at the reception counter so we took two singles, showered and Brian changed into his jeans and boot-scooting boots.

We were hungry. We had eaten nothing apart from a chocolate bar and a chicken pie at Mannum at eleven o'clock. Both of us were dead tired, from thirteen hours of non-stop paddling, into a head wind for most of the day. But we still felt chipper, enjoying a beer to wash down food we bought from the 'Asian Box' shop - the pub meals were done for the day. The Asian owners work late in Murray Bridge, just like they do on

Sundays in Robinvale. Brian even bought noodles which for the life of me I could not understand why.

"I like noodles," he told me.

We were now as happy as pigs in mud, with only 20 kilometres to my car at Tailem Bend, but to all intents and purposes we had made it. The forecast was for rain in the next 24 hours so we discussed the possibility, if it was raining in the morning, to forget the last twenty kilometres.

We went off to bed. I lay there in heaven, floating on a real mattress, half a metre off the ground thinking at worst only 20 kilometres to go. Good God. I have made it! Today had been a long hard day but I did not want to sleep so I lay there cheering on the Murray Bridge hoons roaring up and down the main street, enjoying the noise of trucker's air brakes and the 100 car-goods train rattling by my window at 4am.

In the morning I looked out and saw heavy rain falling. Brian appeared at breakfast wearing his boots and jeans, not his kayak shirt and shorts - he had made the decision for both of us - our paddling days were finished.

On the 9th of March 1830 Sturt had a hunch the river was about to end, which it did, emptying itself into a lake and Sturt, as you would guess, was a happy man. He named it Lake Alexandrina. (And as you Royalists well know, that would be Princess Alexandrina Victoria, who later became Queen Victoria, who ran the show in Britain for over 60 years).

Eventually Sturt and his men crossed the lake and they finally the reached the sea, where Sturt collected a few sea shells. Being a realistic sort of guy he knew (unlike us) that he had no car to drive himself back home, and their *'difficulties were just about to commence.'*

Instead of being helped by the current they *'now had to contend against the united waters of the eastern ranges, with diminished strength,'* that is, they had to row against the current, and they were slightly buggered.

Sturt could see that his men were *'too much exhausted to perform the task that was before them without assistance'*, so he and his side-kick M'Leay would have to *'to take our share of labour at the oars.'*

(This pleased me no end – Sturt finally doing some hard labour - the slacker.)

They started their return trip to Sydney on February 18 1830, and they struggled, as one would expect, rising at dawn, and pulling on the oars until past seven, and often to nine o'clock. He allowed his men only an hour of rest, from half-past eleven to half-past twelve, and it was April 28 before they reached Pondebadgery (near Wagga Wagga). From there Sturt sent a man forward with letters to the Governor, as one did in those days, and Sturt reached finally reached Sydney on May 25 after an absence of nearly six months.

My hat goes off to the man. The local press was impressed too, as they should have been, with the *Sydney Gazette* of Thursday 27 May 1830 giving notice that:

Captain Sturt arrived in town on Monday evening, from his arduous expedition, in excellent health and spirits.

Heading home

Just after breakfast I was in a taxi taking me to Tailem Bend to pick up my car and trailer, and then I picked up Brian and the kayaks from the Murray Bridge Rowing Club. Then we were off to Goolwa for an obligatory photo, and after that we would head for Mildura - where Brian would pick up his car and we would part ways, not to speak to each other for at least 12 months, and for me to never kayak again, ever.

In the car I put on some quality country music on for him, to take his mind off his broken marriage, starting with the classic: 'Thank God and Greyhound she's gone'. I even told him a true story about unfaithful women, or what the Malay people do to an unfaithful woman. Alfred Wallace was in Lombock, an island next to Bali and he was told that for a serious infidelity, a woman and her lover would be tied back to back and thrown into the sea, to be eaten by crocodiles. I suggested that all he needed was to find was a couple of crocs in Tasmania, for revenge.

At Goolwa there was no Mayor in sight, no hero's reception for us, no ovation from the crowds, no flourish of trumpets, just a photo taken by an innocent passer-by and then a hot meat pie in a Goolwa café. We shook hands. We had managed the trip without a 'rupture' of any sort, not even a harsh word. We are close friends, like two peas in a pod.

We were then away from Goolwa, kayaks on my old trusty trailer and heading to Mildura. I was so happy that I was done with kayaking - at that moment, exotic trips down the Seine and the Danube, which had come up in past conversations after a Guinness or two, were all talk. I was looking forward to enjoying the Coffs Harbour beaches and the Bonville bush.

I wondered if our trip had to be some sort of record, like 'the slowest trip down the Murray', although we did not kayak the whole 2500 kilometres, missing 20 kilometres at the end and a few kilometres in Lake Hume and a few more in Lake Alexandrina, but as Brian said - no one will ever know about that.

What did other old-time guys think at the end of their journeys? Darwin, at the end of his five year voyage in the *Beagle* had words to which I could relate. He wrote that a large proportion of his time was '*spent on the water*', like ours. Darwin was not a great fan of the oceans, calling it a '*tedious waste, a desert of water*'. I am not sure I would go so far as to call the Murray a tedious waste but I was very happy to be in a car and not a kayak.

Thesiger, who you may remember joined Brian and I (in print anyway) as we travelled from Swan Hill to Mildura, made these comments after he had travelled across the Empty Quarter of Arabia:

To others my journey would have little importance. It was a personal experience, and the reward had been a drink of clean, nearly tasteless water. I was content with that.

We did better than Thesiger with his drink of water; our reward had been a meat pie at Goolwa.

And just in case you are preparing to take action against me for sexism, owing to the exclusion of any mention of female explorers so far, let me finish with Florence Ninian von Sass, a Hungarian lass who married an Englishman Samuel Baker. In the 1850s these two were in Africa, having a great time searching for the source of the Nile River - they became ill with fever, their baggage animals died, they quelled a mutiny amongst their men, their food supplies failed, a hippopotamus overturned their boat, and generally they found life tough. But they did reach Lake Albert (one of the sources of the Nile), and Samuel wrote at the end of their travels:

Had I really come from the Nile sources? It was no dream.

A witness sat before me; a face still young, but bronzed like an Arab by years of exposure to a burning sun; haggard and worn with toil and sickness, and shaded with cares, happily now past; the devoted companion of my pilgrimage, to whom I owe success and life – my wife.

I glanced across at my paddling partner but he did not look too worn and haggard.

As we travelled along to pick up Brian's car we did not say a great deal. We were lost in our own thoughts. I guessed Brian was day dreaming of his sexy German neighbour or Miss Brown Legs at Tintaldra. No, I was wrong.

267

He interrupted my thinking:

"Hey! I've just remembered. I never did get to see the world's biggest gum tree near Mildura."

Epilogue

Hume, in his 'Statement of Facts' about his travels with Hovell, wrote that: '*I would prefer being rid of him altogether.*'

Now, at no stage did I ever wish to be rid of Brian. He may not have supplied copious quantities of Murray cod for the dinner table, but without his duct taping skills where would we have been?

Sturt, in his account of his travels in his letters to the NSW Governor, had nothing but praise for his right-hand man M'Leay, even in times of trouble:

Amidst these distresses, M'Leay preserved his good humour, and endeavoured to lighten the task, and to cheer the men as much as possible.

I must admit that Brian kept his '*good humour*', in spite of my more than occasional grumbling, and like M'Leay, made every effort to cheer me up, '*as much as possible.*'

Brian's fine attributes must have impressed his next door neighbour, the 10 foot tall German – the last I heard was that he had won her heart.

I made a note to call him, to see how his love life had progressed: in 12 or 18 months time of course.

Bibliography

Austin, J., 'Northanger Abbey.'

Baker R., Baker, M., and Reschke, W., 'Murray River Pilot.'

Baker, S. W., 'The Heart of Africa.'

Čapek, K., 'A Selection of Fables and Would-be Tales.'

Carter, C. R., 'Victoria, the British "El Dorado".

Cherry-Garrard, A.G.B., 'The Worst Journey in the World.'

Cook, F.A., 'Through the First Antarctic Night.'

Darwin, C. R., 'The Voyage of the Beagle'.

Farwell, B., 'A Biography of Sir Richard Francis Burton'.

Flannery, T., 'The Explorers.'

Hovell, W., 'William Hovel Journal.'

Hume, H., 'A Brief Statement of Facts, etc, etc. Expedition from Lake George to Port Phillip in 1824'.

Lee, I,. 'Early Explorers in Australia' quoting Allan Cunningham.

McPherson, Rev,. P., 'Aboriginal Names of Rivers in Australia Philologically Examined.'

Mitchell, T.L., 'Three expeditions into the interior of eastern Australia : with descriptions of the recently explored region of Australia Felix, and of the present colony of New South Wales.'

Raby, P., 'Alfred Russel Wallace: A Life.'

Report of 'AMA and the Australian Doctors Fund on the Australian Constitution, medicine and the law, old Parliament House, Canberra, 7 June 1996', quoting the words of a Dr John Quick at a Corowa meeting in the 1890's, in the move towards Federation.

Right, M., and Kroemer, N., 'Murray River Charts.'

Scott, R.F., 'Scott's Last Expedition, the Journals of Captain R.F. Scott.'

Sturt, C., 'Two expeditions into the interior of southern Australia during the years 1828,1829,1830,1831, with observations on the soil, climate and general resources of the Colony of New South Wales'.

Thesiger, W., 'Desert Sands'.